THE ART OF WAR

SUN TZU

Translated by
Jonathan Clements

Constable • London

CONSTABLE

This translation first published in Great Britain in 2012 by Constable,
an imprint of Constable & Robinson Ltd

3 5 7 9 10 8 6 4

Translation © Jonathan Clements 2012

The moral right of the author has been asserted.

All rights reserved.
No part of this publication may be reproduced, stored in a retrieval system, or
transmitted, in any form, or by any means, without the prior permission in writing
of the publisher, nor be otherwise circulated in any form of binding or cover other
than that in which it is published and without a similar condition including this
condition being imposed on the subsequent purchaser.

A CIP catalogue record for this book
is available from the British Library.

ISBN 978-1-78033-001-3

Printed and bound in Great Britain by
CPI Group (UK) Ltd, Croydon CR0 4YY

Papers used by Constable are from well-managed forests and
other responsible sources

MIX
Paper from
responsible sources
FSC® C104740

Constable
An imprint of
Little, Brown Book Group
Carmelite House
50 Victoria Embankment
London EC4Y 0DZ

An Hachette UK Company
www.hachette.co.uk

www.littlebrown.com

For
Jerome Mazandarani

Contents

Introduction:
Translating *The Art of War*

Supposedly, among the books of ancient China, only Lao Tzu's *Dao De Jing* exists in more translations than *The Art of War*. Sun Tzu has been explained, quoted and rearranged by scholars and soldiers for centuries. In English alone, there are countless editions, each as much a product of its own era as Sun Tzu's.

The Art of War even has to be 'translated' into modern Chinese. Even though the Chinese pride themselves on speaking a 3,000-year-old language, *The Art of War* is difficult for a modern Chinese reader to access directly. There have been radical changes in written grammar over the intervening centuries, particularly amid the modernizing turmoil of the last hundred years, and while the character for 'war' still means 'war', many other ancient symbols have gained new meanings and associations.

To a modern Chinese reader, the original text of Sun Tzu chimes with occasional familiar terms, surrounded by an odd noise of strange symbols and false friends. Just as an English reader faced with Latin might guess that *sol* is something to do with the sun, and a *mons* is a mountain, Chinese readers see recognizable words in ancient texts, although they are often left unsure of their pronunciation or precise meaning. As a result, most modern Chinese editions of Sun Tzu are parallel texts, including the latest agreed 'original' alongside a far wordier gloss in modern Mandarin that fills in the blanks and elucidates particular points.

You need only look at the cover of this book to see the difficulties of translating Chinese from 2,500 years in the past. The author's name was not Sun Tzu. The book's title was not *The Art of War*. And yet those are the terms most recognizable to modern readers, the most popular interpretation of the book called *Bingfa*, credited to the ancient authority whose title would be written in today's Pinyin romanization as Sun Zi.

A modern Chinese reader will intuitively know that a book with the title *Bingfa* is Sun Tzu's *The Art of War*.

But a modern Chinese dictionary generally gives the definition of the component characters as:

> *Bing*: weapons; arms; soldier; rank-and-file soldier; private; army; troops; military; pawn; one of the pieces in Chinese chess.

> *Fa*: law; method; way; follow; model after; standard; model; Legalists; the Legalist School; Buddhist doctrine; the dharma; magic; France.

Neither 'art' nor 'war' is paramount among the possible translations of the component characters. A far more exacting translation of the title might be *Military Models* or *Army Methods*. At no point does Sun Tzu even attempt to suggest that war is an art. Far from it: Sun Tzu regards war as a very distinctive *craft*, a series of vital rules and considerations. It would seem that calling it *The Art of War* is a foreign interpolation, likely an attempt to associate it in the mind of strategists with the sixteenth-century *Dell'arte della Guerra* of Machiavelli.

Variations of the Text

Classical Chinese is a notoriously terse language, and

translators often over-compensate by inserting qualifications and elucidations that either do not really belong, or are appropriate only for certain readerships. As an example, here is the second line of the first chapter of *The Art of War*, summarizing the topics to be later discussed.

故經之以五事校之以計而索其情
一曰道二曰天三曰地四曰將五曰法

Here are just six of the many rival English translations of the *same piece of text*:

Lionel Giles (1910)
The art of war, then, is governed by five constant factors, to be taken into account in one's deliberations, when seeking to determine the conditions obtaining in the field. These are: (1) The Moral Law; (2) Heaven; (3) Earth; (4) The Commander; (5) Method and Discipline.

Samuel Griffith (1963)
Therefore appraise it in terms of the five fundamental factors and make comparison of the seven elements later named. So you may

assess its essentials. The first of these factors is moral influence; the second, weather; the third, terrain; the fourth, command; and the fifth, doctrine.

Thomas Cleary (1988)

Therefore measure in terms of five things, use these assessments to make comparisons, and thus find out what the conditions are. The five things are the way, the weather, the terrain, leadership and discipline.

Ralph Sawyer (1993)

Therefore structure it according to the following five factors, evaluate it comparatively through estimations and seek out its true nature. The first is termed the Tao, the second Heaven, the third Earth, the fourth generals, the fifth the laws for military organization and discipline.

Andrew Zieger (2010)

Classically, there are five things to consider when evaluating and searching out a situation. First is *approach*, second is *heaven*, third is *earth*, fourth is the *general*, fifth is *method*.

Jonathan Clements (2012)
War is governed by five crucial factors,
which you must consider and implement:
- Politics
- Weather
- Terrain
- Leadership
- Training

None of these translations is necessarily 'right' or 'wrong'. Each reflects its author's era and background, and their assumptions about their implied readers. Lionel Giles, out of copyright and hence often the most readily available, is a work of impressive scholarship, but written in a florid Edwardian manner that is often impenetrably obtuse. It is the easiest *The Art of War* to find online, but written in an English that is already outmoded and cluttered. It has been seized upon by certain publishers in search of a free 'classic' to add to their list, and can be found clogging the internet in numerous ebook editions. It is free. You get what you pay for.

The standard version used in military academies is the Oxford University Press edition from 1963, translated by Brigadier General Samuel Griffith (1906–83) as part of his doctoral thesis. This has been recently reprinted in a hardback, partially illustrated version and remains highly regarded. Partly, this is because Griffith was himself a military man, but also a translator who included many commentaries and asides from later Chinese thinkers. For an idea of how *The Art of War* was regarded over the last 1,500 years or so, Griffith offers a valuable inclusion of these commentaries, unsurpassed in English.

As Ralph Sawyer archly (and entirely justifiably) observes, many other translations on the market amount to little more than uncredited reworkings of Giles or Griffith, regardless of the name on the cover. Sawyer's own 1993 version is most useful for its sense of context – *The Seven Military Classics of Ancient China*, includes Sun Tzu as just one thinker among many, demonstrating how other theorists applied his work or contended with it. Following traditional models in Chinese thought, Sawyer places *The Art of War* as one in a continuum of manuals, although many later authors still regarded Sun Tzu as the first and the best. While Sun Tzu's is probably the oldest, Sawyer's line of manuscripts finishes 1,000 years later with *Questions and Replies Between Tang Taizong and Li Weigong* (c. AD 630).

The list goes on, with academically exacting versions from Thomas Cleary and John Minford, also widely available and respected. Roger Ames' *Art of Warfare*

(1994) not only contains a good translation of Sun Tzu's thirteen chapters, but a wealth of ancillary detail and useful footnotes for other translators. For the reader in search of greater detail, not the least of the controversial 'lost' chapters, Ames is recommended among the confusing whirl of available alternatives. Ames includes not only fragments from recent archeological discoveries, but also snippets attributed to Sun Tzu in numerous other books from later centuries. This actually opens a whole new can of worms, as the books quoted seem to be entirely different Sun Tzu works, now lost, such as *The Secret Essentials of the Art of War* (*Bingfa Miyao*), or the *Prognostications of Sun Tzu* (*Sunzi Zhan*).

We should also mention two other Chinese authors whose fates have become entwined with those of Sun Tzu. The infamous *Book of Lord Shang* (c. 330 BC), a book more concerned with Machiavellian politics than war, but which nevertheless applies military ruthlessness to management, is occasionally paired with Sun Tzu in English editions. There is also the work of Sun Bin, supposedly a descendant of Sun Tzu, whose writings are sometimes published in tandem with his, both because of this relationship, but also because he, too, has been augmented by recent archeological discoveries, particularly those in Yinqueshan, discussed in 'The Life and Times of *The Art of War*'.

Some authors, most notably Victor Mair in *Sun Zi's Art of War: Military Methods* (2007), have even suggested that Sun Tzu and Sun Bin are the same person, and that if we are looking for the 'complete' Sun Tzu, we should be looking for it by incorporating the works of this 'other' author. Nor is this a wild fancy; even if Sun Tzu and Sun Bin are not the same person, it is certainly possible that several chapters currently ascribed to Sun Bin may actually have been part of Sun Tzu's *The Art of War*, and were unlucky enough to be in the wrong pile in a certain grave when archeologists unearthed them. This debate over precise authorship continues, politely and carefully, among scholars. Rather than pre-empt a later ruling one way or the other, I have kept to the traditional thirteen chapters of *The Art of War* in my translation.

In more recent times, Andrew Zieger's 'image-for-image' translation (2010) is perhaps the most thought-provoking. It adheres, sometimes brutally, to the original Chinese. It sets the Chinese and English in parallel, and tries, as far as possible, to neither add to nor subtract from the original. It is a fascinating exercise in raw translation, but sometimes wilfully clings to readings known to be incorrect, while on other occasions happily substituting variant characters agreed by other translators to be more likely to be accurate. However, because Zieger's translation is more statistically informed than many others, his notes are able to offer interesting arguments, along the lines of certain problematic characters that have meant one thing in half a dozen other parts of the text, and hence may be presumed to mean the same thing in a place where their meaning is otherwise unclear.

With so many versions of *The Art of War* to choose from already, the reader is sure to ask why the world needs another one. As the sample translation given above should hopefully demonstrate, this version is a gateway text for the contemporary reader, prepared with the newcomer in mind, presenting the bare bones of the famous thirteen chapters in the clearest translation possible. Deeper issues in authorship, reception and translation are saved until after Sun Tzu himself has had the chance to speak – literally.

'Master Sun says . . .'

In approaching a text in Classical Chinese, we must consider the immense differences between books and reading in our time and in that of *The Art of War*. There was, in ancient China, no such thing as our 'book'. Classical Chinese was usually carved onto bamboo strips bound together with leather or string. Their physical appearance was closer to that of a modern rolling window blind than a book. One of the problems faced by modern archeologists is the reconstruction of books from scattered fragments of bamboo – when the leather straps or connecting string decays, ancient Chinese books collapse into hundreds of scattered strips of unpaginated bamboo.

Many translators have overlooked the *performance* required from Classical Chinese texts. Classical Chinese is a literary language that often summarizes the vernacular rather than directly quoting it. The meaning of Classical Chinese has to be unpacked and interpreted. We might consider the written *The Art of War* less as Sun Tzu's book than as his notes for a speech or for further discussion.

The first words of the text, repeated at the head of each chapter, are 'Master Sun *says*'. Everything that follows is implied speech, delivered to an implied listener: a local king perhaps, or a group of officer cadets. This is surely the origin of many of the text's apparent repetitions: not the meanderings of a forgetful author, but moments of call and response by a commanding orator. 'This is how war is waged,' says Sun Tzu at various points, an antiphon to wake up the students at the back, just as he makes an important point. The reader is encouraged to read it out loud; it is often a text better heard than read.

While handmade copies certainly might circulate of the better-known texts, the best way for a ruler to 'read' Sun Tzu was to have Sun Tzu's words spoken, in person, by Sun Tzu himself. It is such interactive performances, in which a monarch might question a philosopher during and after a reading of the philosopher's work, that have generated the many conversations and interrogations that can often be found interpolating classical Chinese texts. There is the original, and then there are the conversations and responses inspired by the original, and then sometimes there is the revised manuscript incorporating such conversations, followed in later centuries by the annotations of others. In such a way, ancient Chinese books often bear a closer resemblance to academic working papers, and are less 'published' than they are placed on a continuum of revisions and facsimiles.

'Everybody else says . . .'

The text of Sun Tzu is not fixed, either. The sparse, blunt, original text is rarely printed unadorned. Instead, over the centuries it has accreted commentary upon commentary by other military men or copyists with points of their own to add. It is not unusual in translations of Sun Tzu to see a single sentence of the original on a page, accompanied by several much longer comments and elucidations by various notables from the dozen or so dynasties that followed the time of Sun Tzu, sometimes even forgetting about him altogether and arguing among themselves.

That is all very well, but it is surely Sun Tzu's original that we want to read, not the marginal annotations of Li Chuan, who has found a quote in another book that is almost the same, or Du You, who thinks he has found an exception to one of the rules. It is possible for a modern edition of Sun Tzu to come so barnacled with commentary that the original is all but lost amid a torrent of qualifications and asides. Jia Lin and Wang Xi, Zhang Yu and Cao Cao, a veritable legion of later generals and experts have had their own comments appended, tagging the brisk, original text with top-heavy explanations, such that in the space of a few centuries, the average size of a copy of *The Art of War* ballooned from the original thirteen chapters to over eighty. Many of these commentators earnestly attempt to update the original text for modern times, when 'modern times' might now be over a millennium in our own past.

Nor are they always notes of wisdom. Some, particularly those of Cao Cao, might be the asides of smart military thinkers. Others seem more like the unwelcome marginalia of whoever had the book last. In particular, one Tang dynasty authority merrily offers earnest theories on what Sun Tzu *may* have meant, sometimes the exact opposite of what is on the page, even if Sun Tzu himself clarifies it a couple of sentences later. In such cases, less is truly more. In the interests of revealing the original, I have stripped most of these interpolations right back – interested readers can find them in Griffith (1963). I have added footnotes of my own, but only to those places where Sun Tzu's meaning is not apparent, or where I have made a translation decision liable to raise eyebrows if left unqualified.

The Life and Times of Sun Tzu

Sun Tzu appears in only a handful of early histories. By the time his name is mentioned in *The Grand Scribe's Records*, an ancient set of annals detailing the history of China before the Han dynasty, he is already a soldier of some renown and so we can only guess at his early life.

There is no definite date of birth or death for Sun Tzu, merely an assertion that he came from the powerful northern state of Qi, the 'Land of the Devout'. Born some time in the mid-sixth century BC, he grew up in a troubled state, riddled with scandals and intrigues. His family name was Sun. His given name in *The Grand Scribe's Records* was supposedly Wu, which conveniently means 'war' or 'martial' and may itself have been a nickname or later identifier. Sun Zi (or Sun Tzu as it is popularly rendered) was merely his title, 'Master Sun'.

There was no such place as 'China' at the time. Instead, a Sovereign Son of Heaven claimed to rule all under heaven. In fact, the Sovereign was the master of little more than a small pocket of land on the banks of the Yellow River, at the centre of a patchwork of far larger dukedoms whose rulers swore fealty to him. The era is known today as the Spring and Autumn Period, the time from 771 BC–403 BC in which the power of the supposed rulers of 'all under heaven' dwindled. The dukes, originally installed as viceroys to carry the ruler's authority to distant marches, gained greater influence as larger estates conquered smaller ones, establishing ancient superpowers with far better resources than the ruler they supposedly served. While the Son of Heaven looked on powerless, the dukes jockeyed for position among themselves, declaring war on each other, often in the Son of Heaven's name, conquering and destroying rival states. Occasionally, a duke would aspire to the position of Hegemon, a prince among princes, understood to be the most powerful of the nobles, and most favoured by the Son of Heaven.

Qi, Land of the Devout, was a dukedom in the north-east, roughly corresponding to modern Shandong. Like all the other dukedoms, it was involved in a series of spats and conflicts with its fellow states, although Qi had internal problems of its own that threatened its security. Around the time that Sun Tzu is presumed to have been born, 555 BC, Qi was invaded by an army from the neighbouring state of Jin.[1]

The reigning duke attempted to flee, died under suspicious circumstances, and was ominously replaced by his son Duke Zhuang (r. 553–548 BC), who had spent several years in Jin as a royal hostage, and who had been recently supplanted in his father's affections by his half-brother. The half-brother pretender was soon executed, and Duke Zhuang soon attracted complaints from his ministers, for demonstrating an unduly friendly attitude towards emissaries from the state that had caused his father's downfall. Before long, he was already pursuing his own agenda, offering sanctuary to a refugee from Jin, and sending his new ally back with military support. If this was an attempt to strike back at Jin, it failed.

The luckless Duke Zhuang seemed adept at creating problems for himself. He developed an intense

---

1 Nienhauser et al., *The Grand Scribe's Records VI: The Hereditary Houses of Pre-Han China Part I by Ssu-ma Ch'ien*, volume I. pp. 96–107 contains the annals of Qi during the supposed period of Sun Tzu's early life.

interest in an unnamed woman of legendary beauty, who came from a domain on the borderlands between the two countries. He made little attempt to conceal their affair, on one occasion even stealing a hat that belonged to the woman's cuckolded husband, and publicly gifting it to a courtier.

By 548 BC, Duke Zhuang's behaviour had created a large enough revolutionary faction to ensure his own demise. The unhappy husband joined forces with a resentful palace eunuch, and, it seems, the mistress herself, ambushing the duke as he sneaked off to one of his trysts. The frantic duke fled by climbing up the terraces of his own palace, but, realizing that he was cornered, begged to be allowed to commit suicide in the palace of his ancestors.

When this request was refused, he made a run for it, sustaining an arrow wound to his leg while trying to clamber over a wall. He fell to the ground and was hacked to death by his subjects.

His chief minister, Yan Ying,[2] was found with the duke's corpse pillowed in his lap, weeping and lamenting the poor quality of Qi's rulers; Zhuang's father had

---

2 See Clements, *Confucius*, pp. 33–42 for some of the apocryphal stories of the feud between Yan Ying and Confucius.

tried to flee the enemy attackers; now Zhuang himself had tried to flee vengeful courtiers, which was even more embarrassing, as they were his own subjects. Now, the cuckolded husband was promoted as the first minister of Qi, under the new Duke Jing (r. 547–490 BC), a second half-brother of the murdered ruler. Two successive chief scribes were executed for faithfully describing the murder of Duke Zhuang in the state annals; the scandal was eventually allowed to stand after the cover-up plainly failed to take hold.

It is odd, if we are to believe assertions of Sun Tzu's origins, that he would have come to prominence in such an environment without attracting the notice of the local chroniclers. *The Grand Scribe's Records* has time to discuss fights over the authorship of a single line in the annals of Qi, as well as the petty fumblings of a lascivious duke, but at no point does it mention the activities of Sun Tzu, supposedly the greatest military leader of his age. The period does not see Qi fighting any truly notable battles, and indeed, the wars that *are* recorded did not go in Qi's favour. If the young Sun Tzu saw service in Qi during this period, then he would have been a witness to a series of defeats and retreats.

Duke Jing reigned for an impressive six decades, although it cannot have seemed at the time that he would last quite so long. At the time of his elevation, the Land of the Devout was still trapped in a whirlpool of scandal. In the decade that followed, a series of palace putsches saw several clans fighting for the chance to be close to the duke.

The duke somehow remained in charge while his ministers knifed and poisoned one another with melodramatic frequency. Similar internal problems beset the neighbouring land of Lu, leading to the arrival of Lu's deposed ruler as a refugee in 517 BC. This is notable for the fact that the fleeing nobleman was accompanied by his own trusted councillor, Confucius – if Sun Tzu were working for Duke Jing at this time, then the two famous Chinese philosophers may have even met.

However, it is more likely that they never did, as Sun Tzu probably left Qi many years before. If we are to trust at all in the contemporary claims of authorship for Sun Tzu, then we must assume that he had long since left Qi, and achieved some degree of fame as a theorist or warrior in some other state. There are numerous events in the historical record that may have propelled Sun Tzu away from his homeland. Perhaps he was involved with one of the many palace factions that duelled over power during the reign of Duke Jing, and escaped to freelance for one of the other dukedoms. He might have even been responsible for some of the defeats suffered by Qi in the period, as an exile advising Yan, the Land of Swallows, which successfully repelled a Qi invasion in the 530s BC. Whatever his activities during his early life, there is no clue of them in the historical record. Sun Tzu, himself, however, would not necessarily regard the lack of his mention in dispatches as proof that he did not exist, noting in his *Art of War*: 'In olden times, the truly skilled warriors won easy victories. Hence, when those skilled warriors were victorious, their wisdom brought them no fame.'

This, then, was the time in which Sun Tzu matured. According to the surviving books that mention him, this was also the period in which Master Sun, a native of the state of Qi, wrote thirteen chapters on martial matters, which made him something of a celebrity. His thirteen chapters travelled considerably more than he did, and somehow made it far to the south, to the upstart state of Wu, near the mouth of what is now the Yangtze River.

Wu was far from the centre of civilization, regarded as something of a barbarian state with only remote connections to the Sovereign Son of Heaven. However, it had a king, and it had wars to fight. Late in the sixth century, the ruler of Wu summoned Master Sun to his domain, and offered him a job.

The Southern State of Wu

The newly crowned king, Helü, had a varied martial reputation. In 525 BC, as a young prince, he had led a disastrous expedition upriver against the powerful neighbouring state of Chu, losing the national flagship in the process. He retrieved his losses in a rematch, using unspecified underhand means, and was back in 519 BC as the leader of a more successful expedition. This second assault saw him meddling in local politics, and leading spin-off invasions of the nearby states of Chen and Cai.

In 518 BC he was back again, as the result of a suspicious escalation of bad feeling from a petty dispute on the borderlands. Two silk-farmers' daughters, one from Wu and another from Chu, had somehow got into a fight over mulberry leaves – their silk-worms' food supply. They were backed up by their families, then by their neighbours, and eventually by their village headmen, who called in state reinforcements. With tensions already high on the border, the lowly spat soon intensified into military action. In the initial skirmish, the Wu girl's hometown was destroyed. Helü's uncle sent in the famously belligerent prince to exact revenge, which he did by seizing two towns across the border.

In February 514 BC, seemingly passed over in military

appointments in favour of other princelings, Helü hatched a plan to kill his uncle the king. He invited him to a dinner party, where a suicidal assassin called Zhuan Zhu managed to stab the king with a knife that had been hidden inside one of the fish on the table, leaving the throne open for the rebellious nephew.

Enthroned as King Helü ('Closed Hut'), the new monarch immediately made a number of controversial appointments. He put several Chu exiles in prominent positions in his administration, including one who had a claim on the neighbouring country's throne. His acts led to a series of putsches in Chu among presumed sympathizers and agents, which only increased the number of vengeful exiles seeking sanctuary in Helü's kingdom.[3]

Helü was a young king with a martial reputation, already seemingly hell-bent on going to war against a massive and antagonistic neighbouring country. It was at this point that he summoned the famous military expert Sun Tzu to him.[4]

---

3 Nienhauser et al, *The Grand Scribe's Records VI: The Hereditary Houses of Pre-Han China Part I by Ssu-ma Ch'ien.* pp. 14–16.

4 Sawyer, *The Seven Military Classics of Ancient China*, p. 151, notes that another ancient text, the *Spring and Autumn Annals of Wu and Yue*, relates a similar story, but describes Sun Tzu as a *native* of Wu.

Helü was clearly an avid fan. 'I have read all your thirteen chapters,' he gushed, telling Sun Tzu that he was very fond of war and all its sport.

This was the wrong thing to say. Like many a fan encountering a lifelong hero, King Helü was in for a series of rude awakenings. Sun Tzu politely but bluntly replied that war was not a game, nor was it something to be 'fond of'. It was a last resort, taken only to ensure the upper hand in an inevitable conflict.[5]

King Helü pressed on regardless, begging Sun Tzu's pardon for only having formerly appreciated the superficial elements of his text. He entreated the military celebrity to show him some of his ideas, perhaps by training a platoon of cadets that was entirely untried.

Sun Tzu agreed, inadvisedly musing that he could essentially train anyone: courtiers, randomly chosen peasants, men or even women. King Helü loved the idea, and immediately volunteered the services of his palace harem.

In a rare moment of retreat, Sun Tzu tried to get out of it, suggesting that the ladies of the court might not have the necessary strength, and that perhaps—

---

5 'An Interview with the King of Wu' from the Yinqueshan manuscripts, in Ames, *Sun-Tzu: The Art of Warfare*, pp. 191–6.

'What could possibly go wrong?' laughed King Helü.[6]

Reluctantly, Sun Tzu got to work, only to discover that King Helü was planning on watching the whole enterprise. Warning the sovereign that boot camp was a long and dull affair, Sun Tzu asked him to go back inside, promising to call him back when the women were sufficiently drilled.

Early in the morning, the women assembled in the hunting park to the east of Helü's palace. His staff sergeant berated the giggling group, making sure that they knew their left from right, and their front from back. He told them of the turns required, and of the drum signals that would order them to turn, march, halt and kneel – vital manoeuvres for contemporary infantry. The kneeling position seems to have been the 'at-ease' stance, allowing soldiers in armour to take some of the weight off their legs while listening to their commander.

Sun Tzu also sternly warned them that they would need to get it right, or their lives would be forfeit. He made three attempts to get the women to rise, march

---

6 '. . . *wei, you he hui hu*?' Literally, 'Have what regrets, eh?' Ames, p. 190.

and halt at the appropriate drum signal, but they continued to bump into each other and laugh at the ludicrous situation.

At that point, Sun Tzu ordered the two company commanders out of the ladies' ranks, made them kneel, and ordered them to be beheaded.

King Helü, contrary to his earlier promise, had come back to observe, and protested that his girls should be given another chance. Clearly not taking things all that seriously himself, he asked that the girls be spared.

Sun Tzu replied by quoting *The Art of War* back at its biggest fan: 'Some orders from your prince should not be followed.'

With that, he gave the word for the two girls to be beheaded. He appointed two new company commanders from the survivors, and ordered the signals to be sounded again.

Suddenly, Sun Tzu's platoon knew their left from right. They marched in locked steps; they turned with each drum signal. Sun Tzu sent a message to King Helü, who seems to have stormed off in anger.

'The soldiers are trained. Your Majesty is invited to inspect them. They are ready for any action Your Majesty cares to order, even to the extent of marching through water or fire.'

The King's reply petulantly ordered Sun Tzu back

to his lodgings, noting that he had no desire to inspect the troops.

'The King likes the words,' noted Sun Tzu, 'but he cannot handle the reality.'

Six days of sulking ensued, until Helü reluctantly admitted that he had got exactly what he asked for.

Two years later, the annals of the state of Wu recorded a new conflict. Helü led a force against the giant state of Chu, in pursuit of two defecting princes. Seizing enemy territory with lightning speed, his general made preparations to advance even further. The next sentence in the annals has Sun Tzu, plainly now part of Wu's military organization, saying that the time was not right, and that Helü should halt his advance where it was.

Sun Tzu is last mentioned in the annals of Wu in the year 506 BC. It is not clear whether he was an active general or a stay-at-home consultant, but his counsel seems to have been greatly esteemed. In 506, a Wu army soundly defeated a force from Chu. The Wu commander, a refugee with a particular grudge against the late monarch who had exiled him, infamously desecrated his enemy's tomb, digging up the dead king and whipping the rotting corpse 300 times. Sun Tzu's thoughts on this distinctly unusual act are not recorded.

King Helü's violent life brought little long-term rewards. Although he soundly defeated forces from Chu and Yue, a prophecy foretold that Yue would avenge itself upon his descendants. Even as Helü celebrated his seizure of new territory on the frontier, he heard that his younger brother had crowned himself king in his absence. He returned to fight a civil war, ousting the usurper but giving Chu vital time to recover and fight back.

In a doomed assault on the barbarian kingdom of Yue in 496 BC, King Helü saw one of the strangest sights in Chinese military history – an advancing company of enemy soldiers that halted before his ranks, drew their daggers, and slit their own throats. This diversion kept his troops so preoccupied that they allowed a surprise attack on their own capital, leading to fighting in which Helü contracted a seemingly minor wound to his finger. It turned septic and eventually caused his death. His son (or grandson) Fuchai swore vengeance on the people of Yue, leading to another round of recriminations and reprisals that would dominate his reign and ultimately lead to his own defeat.

King Fuchai reigned from 495 BC until 473 BC, the year in which a resurgent state of Yue destroyed his kingdom. One of Sun Tzu's former colleagues warned the king of trouble ahead, but was ordered to commit suicide for his pains. He died cursing the kingdom, and asking that his eyes be mounted above the Wu capital's gates so he could watch the inevitable enemy victory.

King Fuchai rose to an unprecedented height, daring even to put himself forward as Hegemon – leading duke of all the kingdoms under heaven, and hence the de facto leader of all China. However, his rise was all too brief, and he was defeated by the very sort of espionage that Sun Tzu had discussed in the final chapter of *The Art of War*.

Despite warnings about the dangers presented by the nearby state of Yue, Fuchai did not destroy it. He was preoccupied with Xi Shi, a Yue woman of legendary beauty sent to him as a distraction by Yue emissaries. Nor did he believe that Yue was a threat, having been encouraged in this course by a minister who was secretly taking bribes from the Yue kingdom. It was precisely the kind of 'embedded agent' that Sun Tzu would have recommended for steering an enemy onto the wrong course of action, and in the end, it cost Fuchai his kingdom.

Fuchai's reign saw numerous battles recorded in the annals, in which Sun Tzu's name is not to be found. Considering that the thirteen chapters of *The Art of War*, representing the presumed culmination of a long career, were already in existence and circulation for

Helü to read in 512 BC, we might assume that the Sun Tzu who served in 506 BC was already an old man. He is certainly not mentioned in the putsches and intrigues that dogged Fuchai's realm during his later years, and was perhaps spared the sight of the military he had built up being run into the ground by a clueless head of state.

Arguably, Sun Tzu's true fame did not arise until long after his death, when his thirteen chapters remained in circulation. While many other military treatises were lost in fires, floods and revolts, Sun Tzu's own somehow survived to become ingrained in the Chinese martial tradition. Centuries after the time Sun Tzu supposedly lived, his thirteen chapters were considered to be one of the cornerstones of the Chinese martial tradition. They became required reading for all military men, and helped shape the course of war in Asia for over 2,000 years.

THE ART OF WAR

CHAPTER ONE

Planning[1]

---

1 When stripped of curlicues and flowery language, the first chapter of *The Art of War* can appear blunt and a little repetitive, more like a questionnaire than a passage of text. It may even have been intended for such a use, inviting officers to engage in the ancient Chinese equivalent of ticking boxes on a form to ensure that they have met all the necessary requirements for victory. Although Sun Tzu allows that local, *tactical* circumstances can throw in unknown variables, these only enter his consideration after he has ruled out a selection of issues in strategy and operations.

Master Sun says:

War is of great relevance to the state. It is a matter of life and death, a path to survival or flight. It cannot be ignored.

War is governed by five crucial factors, which you must consider and implement:

- Politics
- Weather
- Terrain
- Leadership
- Training

Politics is what keeps the people in accord with their leader, supporting him with their very lives, unafraid of danger.

Weather involves the conditions of light and shade, heat and cold, hours and seasons.

Terrain may be near or far, difficult or easy, wide or narrow, and the prospect of life or death.

Leadership considers wisdom, trust, compassion, courage and severity.

Training considers logistics, discipline and protocol.

No leader should be unaware of these five issues. Those who are ignorant of them shall fail. When considering your plans, you should ask:

- Which ruler has the political upper hand?
- Which general is most capable?
- Who is favoured by the weather and terrain?
- Who enjoys the greater efficiency of organization?
- Who has the stronger army?
- Whose officers and men are best trained?
- Who rewards and punishes clearly?

Then you will know who will win and who will lose. A general who follows this plan and implements it is certain to win, and should be deployed. A general who does not listen to this plan or implement it is certain to lose, and should be dismissed.

On hearing these factors, only then should you assess mitigating circumstances. Modify your plans to use situational advantages.

Strategy is a doctrine of deceit. When you are capable, act as if incapable. When you are busy, act as if idle. When you are close, appear to be far away. When you are far away, appear to be close. Show openings to lure your enemy. Feign confusion to capture them. If your enemies are solid, make preparations. If your enemies are strong, retreat. When your enemies are angry, taunt them. When they are modest, make them proud. When they are idle, make them work. When they are united, drive them apart. Attack when they are unprepared. Turn up when they do not expect it. This is how the strategist succeeds, by giving nothing away beforehand.

In the temple before battle, the winners have plans with many merits. The losers have plans with fewer merits. Many merits win; a mere handful do not. If there are no merits at all, how much greater the defeat.[2]

This is what we must consider, to determine who will win and who will lose.

---

2 The chapter's final passage uses the character *suan* (calculate, plot, count) on no less than seven occasions. It refers literally to counting, as officers in a temple chamber would pile up tokens on the floor in reference to the advantages and disadvantages of particular plans. The first chapter of Sun Tzu's book would be familiar to any modern leader, not only in the military arena, but beyond it in management and marketing – any environment where there is ground to be gained and resources to be won. It amounts to a call to assess strengths, weaknesses, opportunities and threats.

CHAPTER TWO

Going to War[1]

_____

1 Sun Tzu suggests a reasonable commitment of men
   and *matériel* for a war in his time. Notably, he does not
   scrimp on operational logistics – instead of simply list-
   ing the composition of an army, he notes that an army
   requires transport for its provisions, and devotes much
   of this chapter to the actual economics of a campaign.
   It is, perhaps, for this reason that many other translators
   have chosen to call this chapter 'Waging War' – with the
   emphasis on the waging.

Master Sun says:

This is how war is waged. With 1,000 swift four-horse chariots, 1,000 armoured wagons, a 100,000 armoured men, food and provisions to travel a 1,000 *li*.[2]

---

2 When Sun Tzu mentions a 'chariot', he is referring to the men and *matériel* that accompany one. A single chariot, in his day, bore three officers, but was accompanied by seventy-two foot soldiers. Each wagon, stocked with food and supplies, came with twenty-five support staff, including five grooms, five valets, ten cooks and five 'who collected firewood' – usually a euphemism for slaves or indentured labour. Hence each chariot-wagon pairing accounted for a hundred men, what the Roman army would have called a 'century'. Sun Tzu's '100,000 men' refers to the total of 1,000 chariot-wagon pairings, not an additional force.

He adds that a standard supply cache is enough to travel '1,000 *li*', using an antiquated unit of measurement sometimes misleadingly translated as a league. At the time he was writing, 1,000 *li* was more like 400 miles, reflecting the relatively small scale of Chinese conflicts. If we assume that the army carried enough with it to both advance and return home, the effective range of Sun Tzu's model army was something like 200 miles, from the moment it left friendly territory until the moment it returned.

This incurs costs at home and abroad, for the entertainment of consultants and visitors, for glue and lacquering materials, for chariot and armour supplies. Only with 1,000 pieces of gold per day to hand, can a general raise such a force of 100,000 men.

When going to war, a victory delayed too long will grind down the men and blunt their ardour. A prolonged siege will sap the men's strength and risks damage to the homeland. With weapons dulled and spirits blunted, strength drained and provisions exhausted, rival rulers will take advantage and launch their own attacks. Even a wise man will not be able to right matters after that.

Thus, while soldiers have heard that it is stupid to move too fast, it is also unwise to take too long. There has never been a long war that worked to the benefit of a kingdom.

Those who do not understand the damage done by war cannot possibly hope to understand how a war might also do good. For the general skilled at war, there should only be a single levy of troops, and no more than one resupply.[3] Bring what you need from home,

---

3 However, Sun Tzu does not suggest that a war should involve a single long march, a battle and a return home. He acknowledges that situations can change, and that a successful army might need to resupply, but only once. After its initial advance, Sun Tzu's modern army needs to achieve a certain level of self-sufficiency, drawing new supplies not from its home base, but from the subdued territory where it finds itself. For if it fails to do so, warns Sun Tzu, the many rival states nearby are sure to see the opportunity to make attacks of their own on the over-stretched homeland.

The nature of the resupply has been a subject of much argument among critics and translators. The original Chinese reads that a good general's army 'does not need a third provisioning' – in other words, it should only be resupplied once. Commentators since Cao Cao (i.e. for the last 1,800 years) have suggested that this means an army should be provisioned as it leaves, and restocked

and take provisions from your enemy. Thus, your army will have enough to eat. Sending forces far away is a heavy expense to the homeland. Meanwhile, a military force nearby will raise prices, and high prices exhaust the wealth of the common people.[4]

---

when it returns home – in other words, that it should not be resupplied at all during the campaign. Even if this is true, it is interesting that Sun Tzu thinks of two provisionings as normal, as if he is preparing leaders for the possibility that a military campaign is not guaranteed to pay for itself. If this is the meaning of the double-provisioning quote, then he deftly warns a ruler that merely because a war is over, military expenditure does not automatically fall. Even a victorious army must still be quartered, restocked and trained.

4 Sun Tzu's comments on the economic effects of military operations still hold true today, both in terms of the cost of protracted wars, and the inflationary effects of military billeting in proximity to civilians. My translation of 'common people' stands in for the original Chinese phrase of *bai xing*, 'the hundred surnames', a poetic term for the general population.

Once impoverished, they are soon forced into service. Their strength drained and livelihood gone, homes are left deserted on the central plains. The cost to the common people will be three-tenths of their worth. For the treasury, the cost for broken wheels and worn-out horses; armour, helmets, arrows and crossbows; lances, shields, spears, and tents; oxen and wagons will amount to four-tenths of their worth.

And so, the wise general takes his food from the enemy. A single cup of enemy rice is worth twenty cups to us. A single bale of hay is worth twenty to us. Killing the enemy requires anger, but capturing enemy *matériel* requires rewards. And so, if ten or more chariots are captured during a battle, give a reward to those who took the first. Replace the flags, banners and signals on their chariots, and use them along with your own. Prisoners should be fed and treated well; you can win over the enemy to gain strength.

In war, victory is the prize, not long campaigns. The wise man knows that the leader of an army influences also the fate of the population at large, and steers his country towards safety or danger.

CHAPTER THREE

Strategies of Attack[1]

---

1 This is perhaps the most quoted chapter of Sun Tzu,
containing as it does his famous aphorism about winning
wars without fighting. Although there is a brief treatment
of the logistics of undertaking a campaign in the style of
the previous chapter, this is merely a reminder that wars
are costly enterprises. Sun Tzu is much more interested
here in pure strategy: in the many ways that war can be
avoided through politics, diplomacy and skulduggery.

Master Sun says:

This is how war is waged. It is better to take a kingdom whole than to destroy it. It is better to take an army whole than to destroy it. It is better to take a battalion, a company or a platoon whole than to destroy them. It is not the pinnacle of martial achievement to fight and win a hundred battles. It is the pinnacle of martial achievement to win without fighting.

The greatest form of soldiery is to disrupt your enemy's plans. In descending order, the next best options are:

- disrupting his communications
- confusing his soldiers
- and only then, attacking his cities

Attack his cities only when there is no alternative. Preparing your screens, your chariots and wagons, your tools, weapons and engines, will take three months. Reaching his battlements will take another three months. If the attack is unsuccessful, even the general who drives his men to swarm like ants will lose one-third of his force, and find that the walls still hold. A siege is a disaster.

And so, the skilled general will subdue his enemy without fighting, overcomes the walls without an attack, overthrows the kingdom without delay. He should certainly use every ruse under heaven, so that his army is unstoppable and his advantage complete. Such is the strategy of attack.[2]

---

2 'Under Heaven' (*tian xia*) is a poetic Chinese term for the entire world, usually found in descriptions of the authority of the Son of Heaven. Here Sun Tzu uses it to emphasize the need for a good general to use any possible means to gain an advantage.

This is how you fight:

- When you outnumber ten to one, surround.
- When you outnumber five to one, invade.
- When you outnumber two to one, attack.
- When you are equally matched, divide his forces.
- When you are outnumbered, defend.
- When you are heavily outnumbered, escape.

A small opponent might be resolute, but the larger opponent will still capture him.

The general is the protector of the nation. If he has no weakness, the nation will be strong. If he is flawed, then the nation will be vulnerable. The prince/lord[3] can compromise his general's plans in three ways:

- Ordering him to advance or retreat when such

---

3 Sun Tzu boldly lists the way that management, particularly in the form of a clueless ruler, can interfere with military operations. He uses the term 'prince/lord' (*jun*) because at the time he wrote, China still officially had a figurehead sovereign, and the various separate states were, at least officially, merely dukedoms or princedoms under his central authority. The ruler was known as the 'Son of Heaven', but had a temporal power more akin to that of the Secretary-General of the United Nations than an actual despot. During the Spring and Autumn Period, his power was gradually eroded, and he remained powerless as his dukes fought among themselves, and eventually proclaimed themselves as kings in their own right. One king, the ruler of the westernmost state of Qin, would eventually proclaim himself to be the conqueror of all these kingdoms, choosing for himself the title of First Emperor of China. It is for this reason that I have avoided using the term 'emperor' when referring to the topmost authority in Sun Tzu's time.

an action is impossible. This hobbles the army.[4]

- Interfering in military affairs that he does not understand. This confuses the ranks.
- Making command decisions that he does not understand. This brings doubt to the officers.

With such doubt and confusion in your organization, rivals will soon add to your difficulties. It is said that strife in an army will sap its victory.[5]

---

4 For 'hobbles the army', Sun Tzu uses the word *mi*, which means to tie up an ox or horse to a post. Here he likens the army to a beast of burden, physically prevented from carrying out impossible orders.

5 In a passage aimed not so much at generals but at their civilian superiors, he cautions against treating a military institution as if it is another government office or a democracy. Officers need clear orders and goals, not foggy debates and vague aspirations. Many of Sun Tzu's later commentators would note that the worst damage to a military organization can be done to it by incorrect assumptions made by civilians in powerful positions.

And so, there are five points to knowing victory:

- Win by knowing when to fight and when not to fight.
- Win by knowing how to use both large and small forces.
- Win by uniting both upper and lower ranks in one accord.
- Win by lying in wait for the opponent who is unprepared.
- Win by being an able general without interference from his ruler.

Such are the five principles to knowing victory. And so it is said:

> Know the enemy and know yourself, and in a hundred battles there will be no danger.

> Know not the enemy yet know yourself, and you shall win half your battles.

> Know neither the enemy nor yourself, and you shall surely lose every fight.

CHAPTER FOUR

Disposition

Master Sun says:

In ancient times, the skilled warrior first ensured that he could not lose, then waited for the enemy to bring him victory. I can make myself invulnerable, and wait for the enemy to help me win, but this outcome relies on the enemy. The skilled warrior cannot be defeated, but he cannot necessarily defeat the enemy, either. And so, we say that victory can be understood, but still not achieved.

Making your own defeat impossible requires defence, while achieving victory requires attack. Defend when you are at a disadvantage. Attack when you have the advantage. Those skilled in defence burrow deep into the earth. Those skilled at attack sweep down from the heights of heaven. Thus, victory is certain if you can keep yourself safe.[1]

---

1 This chapter is oddly thick with poetic phrases, including the 'nine earths . . . and nine heavens' (*jiu di jiu tian*) glossed in my translation as simple 'depths and heights', as well as out-of-character poetic sarcasm from Sun Tzu, as he makes wry jibes about fame and celebrity.

There is no achievement in seeing a victory that any man can see. Nor is there glory in winning such a victory that all under heaven speak of your skills, as no strength is involved to lift autumn fluff, as no insight is needed to tell the sun from the moon, as no sharp ears are needed to hear a clash of thunder.[2]

---

2 Sun Tzu is at his best, and arguably his most modern, here when he criticizes the implicit demand among his audiences for narrative tales and military drama. Where a battle's outcome is obvious, there is no evidence of true martial skills on the part of the victor – that much is clear. But Sun Tzu is far more incisive in his rejection of the opposite. There is, he argues, nothing to boast about if you have won a hard-fought battle after many tribulations. If you have had to struggle for your victory, then you have done something wrong.

Sun Tzu is not suggesting that soldiers should not work hard at their profession. But he is reminding his readers of his earlier comments about the undesirability of war. In the interests of self-preservation, he counsels only fighting when one is sure of victory. In the interests of ensuring victory, he counsels endless training, clear command structures and acceptance that war is only a last resort. Moreover, he warns that war is not an enterprise in the pursuit of glory, and that its very best practitioners are likely to be anonymous, invisible and uncelebrated.

In olden times, the truly skilled warriors won easy victories. Hence, when those skilled warriors were victorious, their wisdom brought them no fame. Their courage brought no honour. They fought battles without mistakes. Without mistakes, victory was certain, for the enemy had already lost.

And so, the skilled warrior only stands on ground where he cannot lose, and where he can only cause the enemy's downfall. For the victorious army first arranges its victory, and only then begins battle. A losing army begins battle, and only then attempts to win.

The skilled warrior cultivates this approach, and maintains safeguards and discipline. And so he may steer wins and losses by management:

- Commitment
- Numbers
- Supplies
- Comparisons
- Victory

The terrain determines the commitment. Commitment affects your numbers. Numbers affect your supplies. Supplies affect the comparison of your forces. The comparison of your forces sways your victory.

And so, the victorious army is like a brick weighed against a speck. The losing army is like a speck weighed against a brick. Such is the balance of victory for the fighting man. Like pent-up water dropping a thousand fathoms into a gorge. That is disposition.[3]

---

3 The term 'fathom' is a rough English equivalent to the *ren*, an ancient Chinese measurement of roughly eight feet. The same measurement turns up in the next chapter.

CHAPTER FIVE

Momentum

Master Sun says:

Managing a multitude should be the same as managing a small number. If numbers are divided, fighting a multitude should be like fighting a small force; this is a matter of formations and signals. A large force can surely withstand against the enemy and stay undefeated through the application of the ordinary and the extraordinary.[1]

Your army should move as a millstone crushing an egg, the solid against the hollow. Generally, use ordinary forces to join a battle, and extraordinary forces to win it. And so, the skilled application of the extraordinary is as boundless as heaven and earth, as inexhaustible as rivers and streams, ending only to begin again, like the sun and the moon, dying only to live again like the four seasons.

---

1 For 'ordinary and extraordinary' the original text has *qi zheng*, which might be more normally translated as 'the strange and the true'. Some other translators have chosen variations on 'surprise and expectations'.

There are only five notes on a scale, but those five notes can be varied more times than it is possible to ever hear. There are no more than five colours, but they can combine to greater variation than can be seen. There are no more than five tastes, but they combine to form more flavours than can be tasted.

Permutations in battle arise from nothing more than the ordinary and the extraordinary. But the ordinary and extraordinary combine in more ways than can ever be known. Each brings on the other, like a circle without end. Who can exhaust the possibilities?

It is like the tumble of rocks in fast-flowing waters, set to motion by momentum. It is like the swoop of a diving falcon, that strikes and kills at the critical moment.[2]

And so, for the skilled warrior, momentum should be focused, and timing swift. Momentum is like a drawn crossbow, timing like the released trigger.

---

2 For 'momentum' (*shi*), I have sometimes used the alternative translation of 'permutation'. Other dictionary definitions include 'power, force or tendencies'.

In the tumult and confusion, in the chaos of battle, he is not confused. In the mud and clamour, his formations wheel, but they cannot be defeated. Chaos begets order. Fear begets courage. Weakness begets strength.

Between order and chaos, there is calculation. Between courage and fear there is momentum. And so, he who is skilled at manipulating the enemy creates formations that draw the enemy in. He gives what the enemy will certainly take, and so lures him onward, his own soldiers lying in wait.

The skilled warrior looks to apply mass momentum, so as not to rely on individual men. He chooses men who can use momentum. Using momentum for men in battle is like rolling logs and rocks. Logs and rocks are at peace on flat ground, but dangerous on a slope. They stop on corners, but roll on curves. And so the skilled warrior fights with the momentum of his men. Like a rock rolling down a thousand-fathom mountain, such is that momentum.

CHAPTER SIX

The Weak and the Strong[1]

---

1 Or more literally, the 'hollow and the solid', alluding to the previous chapter's discussions of the relative strengths of an egg crushed by a millstone.

Master Sun says:

He who is first to the field of battle has the luxury of waiting for his enemy. He who is late to the field of battle must rush to either fight or dig in. And so the skilled warrior decides for his foe, and does not permit his foe to decide for him. He may summon the enemy to him by offering a lure, and he may push his enemy back by causing him harm. If an enemy is resting, he may force him to labour. If sated, he can cause him hunger. If at rest, he can force him to move.

Appear where your foe must hurry to meet you. Move swiftly to where you are least expected. You may march 1,000 *li* without tiring, by marching through places that are unoccupied. An attack that is certain to succeed is an attack against an undefended site. A defence that is sure to repel is from an invulnerable site.[2]

---

2 A thousand *li* may simply be a random superlative, or may relate directly to the same distance described in the first chapter. A thousand *li*, we might remember, is 400 miles – Sun Tzu's estimate of the effective range of a normal military force in his era. Here, he reminds his audience that an army need not fight every step of the way, but that it is surely easier to save its strength for the battle that really matters. Far better to appear out of nowhere, perhaps even striking from an allied territory closer to the target. It would be in such cases, in particular, that Sun Tzu's army would require its budget 'for the entertainment of consultants and visitors', as mentioned in Chapter Two.

And so the skilled attacker leaves his enemy unsure of what needs to be defended. The skilled defender leaves his enemy unsure of what needs to be attacked. Subtle beyond subtle, let nothing be seen by observers. Divine beyond divine, let nothing be heard by listeners. By this means, may you control your enemy's fate.

Advance without delay, by rushing towards the weak point. Retreat without pursuit, by moving too fast to be caught. And so, when we desire to fight, even though our enemy is behind a high rampart or deep ditch, he cannot help but engage, because we have attacked the place where he must send help.

When we do not desire to fight, although a line drawn on the ground is our only defence, the enemy will not engage us, because we have lured him away. And so, the foe's disposition is known, and ours is not; while we are united, he is divided. United, we act as one. Divided, he acts in tenths. And our whole force attacks a single point, our multitude against his reduced force.[3]

Where a multitude may strike against a few, I say that this is the place to engage, where he is compromised.

3 Switches in pronouns in this chapter are present in the original, with general statements of fact suddenly replaced with Sun Tzu speaking in the first person, of what 'we' can do, instead of the previously mentioned, hypothetical 'skilled warrior'.

We seek to fight in places that are unforeseen. Not knowing our plans, the enemy must make ready in many places. And while he makes many preparations, we seek to engage where he is at his weakest. And so a ready front weakens the rear. A ready rear weakens the front. A ready left flank weakens the right. A ready right flank weakens the left. And if he tries to defend everywhere, he will be weak everywhere.

The few must make ready for attack. The many make others to make ready for them. And so, he who knows the time and place of battle can march 1,000 *li* and fight. He who does not know the time and place of battle has a left flank that cannot aid the right, and a right flank that cannot aid the left, a front that cannot aid the rear, and a rear that cannot aid the front, be it many tens of *li* away, or only one!

If we look at the men of Yue, their army seemed to be great, but that would not help them win. And so we said that we could bring victory, for although an enemy may be many, he can be rendered powerless.[4]

And so we scheme to see the rights and wrongs in his evaluations. We provoke, to know which of his

---

4 This sudden reference to the 'men of Yue' is an intriguing part of the text, as it seems to be addressed directly to King Helü, the ruler of Wu, who legendarily hired Sun Tzu to help him with his ongoing conflicts against the neighbouring land of Yue. But according to the biography of Sun Tzu in *The Grand Scribe's Records*, and indeed in several fragments from the 1972 Yinqueshan findings, Helü's first words to Sun Tzu were 'I have read all your thirteen chapters'. Either *The Grand Scribe's Records* is wrong about the nature of the chapters that circulated during the life of Sun Tzu, or some or all of this chapter was not part of the original thirteen.

principles are firm or mobile. We compare to know the good or bad conditions in his land.[5] We observe, to know which of his positions are overly fortified or undermanned.

And so army deployments are at their pinnacle when they appear formless. Without form, not even an embedded spy can observe you. Not even a wise man could plot a counter-move. Obvious deployment is an error that can wrest victory from a multitude, although the multitude will not understand why.

5   For my 'good and bad conditions', the original text has *shi sheng*, literally 'death and life'. The same phrase is used at the close of the chapter to refer to the waxing and waning of the moon, and hence is clearly intended by Sun Tzu to refer to changes in circumstance.

Men know that I win through tactics, but they do not know how it may be so. In battle, victories do not repeat themselves. Adjust your tactics all the time. An army formation is like water. As water rushes from the heights to the lowest depths, an army wins by avoiding the strong and targeting the weak. As water is made by terrain to flow in certain ways, so an army must flow with the enemy's situation.

And so, an army does not gain momentum by using the same formations. He who can adapt with the enemy's variations will seize victory and be spoken of as a god.

And so, among the five elements, no one is dominant. Among the four seasons, none is ever present. Days can be short and long. The moon waxes and wanes.

CHAPTER SEVEN

Deployment

Master Sun says:

This is how war is waged. The general receives orders from his prince, recruits the army and assembles the forces. He ensures all is well and pitches his camp. But nothing is more difficult than army deployment.

Army manoeuvres are difficult because they must make the obscure plain and create opportunity from setbacks. And so, you take a long road, but entice your enemy with lures. Although you set off late, you still arrive early. He who knows how to do this knows schemes of the hidden and the plain.

An army manoeuvre that brings advantage may be dangerous. If the entire army sets off on a manoeuvre, it may not arrive in time. When only the soldiers are sent on a manoeuvre, they may lose their equipment. And so when the men leave behind their heavy armour, rushing without rest for day and night, rushing at double the pace, for 100 *li* in order to gain an advantage, your three generals might be captured. For the fierce troops will go ahead, and the hesitant will drop back, such that by this method, only one in ten will arrive.

When an advantage requires a deployment over fifty *li*, you might lose a senior officer, as only half will arrive.

When an advantage requires a deployment over thirty *li*, only two-thirds will arrive.

Besides, an army without equipment is lost. Without provisions, it is lost. Without supplies, it is lost.

And so, if you do not know an ally's strategies, you cannot form an alliance with him. If you do not know the mountains and forests, the choke-points in passes or the boggy ground in marshes, you are unable to set your army in motion. If you do not use local guides, you cannot use the terrain to your advantage.

And so, war stands on deception. Move with the advantage, disperse or concentrate as situations change. When swift, be like the wind. When at rest, be like the forest. When raiding, be like fire. When immobile, be like a mountain, and as inscrutable as shadow. When in motion, be like lightning.

When you plunder, divide the spoils. When you seize territory, divide the profits. Deliberate before moving. First know the hidden and the plain in your calculations, and you will be victorious. That is the art of army deployment.

The Book of Military Administration says: 'When one speaks and is not heard, bring gongs and drums. When one looks and does not see, bring flags and banners.'

And so, for night fighting, use gongs and drums. For fighting during the day, use flags and banners. Thus, you will command the ears and eyes of your men as one. When the men are united, the brave will not advance alone, nor will the cowardly retreat. Such is the way that you use the multitude.

So it is that a whole army may be robbed of its vigour. A general may be robbed of his resolve. At dawn, the spirit is homeward bound. After noon, the spirit dulls. At dusk, spirits revert. The skilled warrior avoids those whose spirits are keen, but attacks those who are dull or homeward bound. That is how one manages ardour.

Orderly in the face of chaos, calm in the face of commotion, this is how one manages the heart.

Close by, awaiting the enemy's march from afar, at rest, while the enemy labours, well fed while the enemy hungers. This is how one manages strength.

Do not attack well-aligned banners. Do not attack serried ranks. This is how one manages variations.

This is how war is waged. Do not turn against those on higher ground. Do not resist those whose backs are against a hill. Do not pursue those who feign retreat. Do not attack keen soldiers. Do not take military bait. Do not obstruct a retreating unit. When surrounding a unit, be sure to leave an escape. If they are ready to fight to the death, do not press too hard.[1]

This is how war is waged.

---

1 For 'feign retreat', the text has *yang bei*, literally 'feign north'. The word in Chinese for 'north' also means 'back' – the back of a correctly positioned house faces north. In this case, troops show their backs, or retreat by running away instead of making a fighting withdrawal.

CHAPTER EIGHT

Variables[1]

---

1 The title of this chapter in the original is *Jiu Bian*, or *The Nine Variations*. Sawyer (1993) suggests these nine variations are given within the text, and applies them to 'terrain', which is not specified in the original. Giles (1910) thinks this chapter refers to nine variations in 'tactics' – an unhelpful gloss, since *most* of the book is about tactics! In fact, the nine variations are neither specified nor directly enumerated in the original text – this is a far cry from the specific numbering that Sun Tzu employs elsewhere. This all serves to give the impression that this chapter is muddled, corrupt or based on unfinished notes.

Master Sun says:

This is how war is waged. The general receives order from his prince, recruits the army and assembles the forces.[2]

- Where terrain is difficult, do not camp.

- Where terrain is open, make alliances.

- Where terrain is isolated, do not wait.

- Where terrain is surrounded, make plans.

- Where terrain is deadly, fight.

- Some roads must not be taken.

- Some troops should not be assaulted.

- Some cities should not be attacked.

- Some terrain should not be contested.

---

2 The opening sentence repeats that of Chapter Seven.

Some orders from your prince should not be followed.

And so, the general who uses these nine variations knows how to wage war. A general who does not use the nine variations, even if he knows the lie of the land, will not be able to use the terrain to his advantage. The leader of an army who does not know the craft of these nine variations, even if he knows the five contingencies, will not be able to use his men well.[3]

---

3 It might appear at first glance that there are *ten* variations here, and indeed, this is how it appeared for many hundreds of years. However, the admonition not to follow the instructions of one's superiors is intended to apply only when the previous nine situations occur. Griffith (1963) suggested this as a fix, but was not proved right until the late twentieth century, when one of the Yinqueshan fragments was found to explain that 'if the commands of your ruler conflict with these ... contingencies, do not obey him.' (See Ames 1993: p. 180.)

And so the wise man in his deliberations is sure to consider the opportunities and the threats. By seizing the opportunities, a mission is sound. By understanding the threats, misfortune can be averted.

Weaken your rivals by doing them harm. Busy your rivals with activity. Confound your rivals with distractions.

This is how war is waged.[4]

---

4 Considering that the phrase 'This is how war is waged' suddenly crops up in the middle of the chapter, the chance remains that this is two chapters that have somehow been conflated. Certainly, the first half seems concerned solely with topographical issues, while the second half suddenly veers on to a discussion of the characteristics of the general. Sun Tzu began Chapter One by suggesting that he would talk about five crucial factors. It is my belief that this chapter may constitute an accidental muddle of what was once intended to be pieces of other chapters on *Terrain* and *Leadership*.

Do not trust that they will not come. Trust that you will be ready if they do.

Do not trust that they will not attack. Trust that you are unassailable if they do.

For the general, there are five dangers:

- If reckless, he may be killed.
- If timid, he may be captured.
- If quick to anger, he may be provoked.
- If proud, he may be humiliated.
- If kind-hearted, he may be guilted.

These five factors are, for a general, indulgences that bring disaster when waging war.

When an army is routed, its leader slain, it is surely due to these five dangers. They cannot be ignored.[5]

---

5   Unfortunately, it's not all that clear what the 'five contingencies' are. They may be the character flaws listed later in the chapter as the 'five dangers', but in which case, why didn't Sun Tzu call them that? A thousand years after Sun Tzu, the Tang dynasty author Jia Lin suggested that the 'five contingencies' were elements that could not be predicted in advance:
   *   Ambush: do not take the short road if there is danger.
   *   Suicidal Bravery: do not attack a foe in dire circumstances, who will fight to the death.
   *   Competence: do not attack a city that is well provisioned and defended by a wise commander leading elite troops.
   *   Compromised Assets: do not fight over terrain that will be hard to defend once taken.
   *   Bad Orders: do not follow the distant ruler's command if it is misguided.
   The fragments of Sun Tzu's alleged descendant Sun Bin, uncovered at Yinqueshan in 1972 after being lost for 2,000 years, mention 'five advantages':
   *   Win by gaining your lord's trust, and an independent command.
   *   Win by knowing the art of war.
   *   Win by enjoying the full support of your men.
   *   Win by having an efficient command structure.
   *   Win by assessing and using terrain to your advantage.

CHAPTER NINE

On the March

Master Sun says:

And now to the matter of locating your forces and observing your enemy.

Crossing mountains, rely on valleys. Camp on high, facing south, so that in battle there is no need to climb further. This is how you position your army in mountainous regions.[1]

Crossing water, be sure to move away from it. If your enemy crosses water to face you, do not meet him in the shallows. Let half of his force be ferried, and then attack for the advantage.

---

1 For 'facing south', the original has *shi sheng*, literally 'seeing growth', i.e. facing the area where plant-life has flourished better.

When readying for battle, do not stay near the water to face your foe. Camp on high ground, in the sun. Do not face a foe who is upstream. This is how you position your army near water.

Crossing salt marshes, do not linger, get out fast. But if your foe attacks while you are in the marsh, be sure to take cover in the reeds, and keep the trees to your rear. This is how you position your army in marshland.

On level ground, position on a gentle slope, with the right flank and rearguard towards the high ground. So that death is before you, but life behind. This is how you position your army on flat ground.

Generally, these forms will bring you the upper hand. It is how the Yellow Sovereign won against his four opponents.[2]

---

2 I have translated *di* here as 'Sovereign', in the understanding that all rulers of China before the famous First Emperor, be they legendary or honorary, could not, by definition, have been 'emperors', at least as we understand the term in English. The Yellow Sovereign was a legendary ruler of China who taught prehistoric man how to tame animals and grow crops. He supposedly defeated four other demigods: the Red Sovereign of the South, the Blue Sovereign of the East, the Black Sovereign of the North, and the White Sovereign of the West. Although our extant text of Sun Tzu's thirteen chapters rarely gives specific examples, one of the Yinqueshan fragments describes a 'Master Sun' – Sun Tzu or Sun Bin – discussing the Yellow Sovereign's legendary battle with the Red Sovereign. This suggests that a larger text by a 'Master Sun' went into far greater depth about the tactics of the days of legend. (See Ames 1993: pp. 182–4.)

Armies like the high and hate the low; they prize sunlight and despise shadow. Secure positioning also fosters health. An army lacking a hundred diseases is said to be sure of victory.[3]

---

3 'hundred diseases' here is *bai ji*, 'the hundred sicknesses', with *bai* (100) here intended in its ancient metaphorical sense of 'too many to count'. There is a vestige of this classical high number in the modern Chinese term for a department store: *baihuo dailou*, or 'great building of a hundred commodities'.

Be sure to set up with a mound, hill, dike or embankment, in sunlight, to your back and rear. This gives advantage to the army, with the terrain as their assistant.

When there is rain upstream, the waters froth. Halt if crossing, and wait for them to settle.

In deep, 'heavenly' torrents, wells, prisons, cages, sinks or fissures, be sure to leave immediately. Do not approach them. We move away from these, and the foe goes near. We should face them, and the enemy should have them at his back.[4]

---

4 Sun Tzu's description of river gorges using a series of forgotten poetic names, *tian jing* (Heaven Well), *tian lao* (Heaven Prison), *tian luo* (Heaven Net), *tian xian* (Heaven Sink), *tian xi* (Heaven Fissure). Around AD 200, some seven centuries after the time of Sun Tzu, the warlord Cao Cao wrote a commentary on the *Art of War* in which he explained them as follows:

- Heaven Torrent: rapids surrounded by high mountains
- Heaven Well: low ground surrounded by mountain heights
- Heaven Prison: terrain at the bottom of the gorge 'like a covered cage'
- Heaven Net: a gorge where troops can be hemmed in and cut off
- Heaven Sink: a sunken gorge
- Heaven Fissure: road at the bottom of a narrow gorge

He who nears narrow defiles or rough ground, lakes or ponds, rushes or reeds, mountains or forest or dense scrub, should conduct prudent and repeated searches, for such are ideal locations for ambush or scouts.

When your enemy is close by but still quiet, he presumes that he has the strategic advantage. When your enemy is far away but calling you to battle, he desires you to make the advance. If he is dug in on gentle terrain, the advantage is his.

The term 'Heaven' not only evokes the upward gaze of the troops in such a gorge, but also the likely direction from which an enemy attack is likely to come in such situations.

When the trees move, he is coming. Where obstacles appear in the thick grasses, he hopes to mislead you. If birds take flight, it means ambush. If beasts stampede, it means a surprise attack.

If dust is high and narrow, chariots approach. If dust is low and wide, infantry approaches. If scattered in pockets, they are collecting firewood. If patchy and intermittent, they are pitching camp.

When he speaks humbly but continues to make preparations, he plans to advance. Where he speaks arrogantly but continues to advance, he plans to fall back. When he suggests a truce without a treaty, he is planning something.

When the light chariots come forward at the flanks, he is forming up. When there is rushing and running and soldiers falling to, it is time.[5]

When half advance and half retreat, it is a trap.

When they stand but lean on their spears, they are hungry. When those who draw water are first to drink it, they are thirsty. When they see an opportunity but do not advance, they are tired. When birds flock, your enemy has broken camp.

---

5   I have followed Griffith (1963) and some other translators in moving the line about the movement of light chariots so that it is placed with discussions of other manoeuvres, thereby keeping all the political discussion in one place. This shift is also commonplace in many modern Chinese editions.

When there are shouts in the night, they are afraid. When there is disorder in the army, the general lacks authority. When flags and signals shift, there is discord. When officers are angry, they are tired.

When they feed grain to the horses and eat meat themselves, when they do not stow cooking utensils or return to camp, they are determined to fight to the death.[6]

When there are whispers, and nods, and quiet words among the troops, your enemy has lost his men.

When there are frequent rewards, he is hard-pressed.

When there are frequent punishments, he is collapsing.

When they are first violent but then fearful, the army has lost its spirit.

When envoys come with kind words, the enemy hopes for a respite.

---

6 The meaning apparent in 'eating meat' implies that the soldiers have slaughtered their oxen in order to make one final feast. Without the oxen, they have no ability to pull their heavier wagons away from the camp, and so plainly do not expect to retreat. It has a resonance equivalent to 'burning one's boats' in the European tradition.

If an enemy force draws up for a prolonged period, angry but not engaging, and not withdrawing, this must be examined with extreme caution.

An army that is not greater in number than its opponent need not be insufficient. We need not advance direct, but merely concentrate our strength and draw reinforcements. He who unthinkingly belittles his opponent is sure to end up a captive.

If soldiers are not yet devoted to you, they will become disobedient when punished. If disobedient, they are difficult to employ. If soldiers are devoted to you and punishment is not meted out, they cannot be employed.

And so, those who combine protocol and discipline are said to be sure to win. When discipline is habitually enforced, the men soon learn obedience. When discipline is habitually disregarded, the men soon learn disobedience. The enforcement of discipline benefits both the army and the officers.

CHAPTER TEN

Terrain

Master Sun says:

Terrain can be:

- Accessible
- Compromised
- Level
- Confined
- High
- Remote

If we can set up but he can still approach, it is Accessible. With the accessible form, first take a high position in the sun. This benefits your *matériel* during battle, and brings an advantage.

If we can enter but retreat is difficult, this is Compromised. With the compromised form, it may be possible to make a surprise attack against an unprepared enemy, and so gain victory. However, if the enemy seems prepared and your attack is unsuccessful, retreat is difficult and you will be at a disadvantage.

If we approach with no advantage, but our enemy also approaches with no advantages, this is Level. With the level form, even if we have the edge on the enemy, we do not approach. Instead, we withdraw to lure him out. When half the enemy have approached, we strike, thus gaining better advantage.

With the Confined form, if we are first on the scene, we should certainly dig in and await the enemy. If the enemy seems to have dug in first, do not attack. If he has not dug in, attack.

With the High form, if we are first on the scene, be sure to take a high sunny position and await the enemy. If the enemy seems to have arrived first, lure him down by pulling back, but do not advance.[1]

With the Remote form, assuming neither of you has the upper hand, it is difficult to begin battle. Battle itself does not bring advantage.

Such are the six approaches to terrain. It is a general's duty not to ignore them.

---

1 For 'High' the original text has *jian* or *xian*, meaning a narrow point, mountain pass or point of danger. Sun Tzu could mean an important strategic nexus: a bridging point, crossroads or other key area, but I have followed Giles (1910) in assuming that it refers specifically to mountain ridges.

The troops may be prone to:

- Desertion
- Insubordination
- Subversion
- Disorder
- Chaos
- Rout

These six conditions are not natural occurrences, but the result of a general's failures.

All things being equal:

If attacking a force ten times your size, you invite Desertion.

If the men are strong but the officers weak, you invite Insubordination.

If officers are strong but the men are weak, you invite Subversion.

If senior officers are angry and disobedient, and pre-emptively make personal sallies against the enemy, the general will be unsure in his commands, and there will be Disorder.

If a general is weak and undisciplined, and does not make his commands clear, then the officers and troops will be unreliable, and the ranks slow to form up. You invite Chaos.

If a general is unable to assess his enemy, ordering a small force against a multitude, or weak forces against the strong, without the best men in the front line, there will be a Rout.

Such are the six approaches to defeat. It is a general's duty not to ignore them.

Terrain should be the ally of an army. Assess your enemy to manage victory. Evaluate choke-points and level ground, far and near. That is the manner of a general at the front.

Know this in battle and victory is certain. Ignore this in battle, and defeat is certain.

And so, when victory is certain but the lord orders you to stand down, make battle unavoidable. When the approach favours defeat, but the lord orders you into battle, make battle impossible.[2]

---

2 Suddenly, the text veers off the point again, discussing the disasters that might befall the troops. But the chapter's name is clearly 'Terrain', and has been for the last 2,000 years – either the chapter has been mislabelled, or this errant passage is another fragment from the otherwise missing chapters on leadership or training.

And so, do not march in search of fame. Do not retreat in fear of dishonour. But keep your men safe, and bring the best advantage to your superiors, that you may be a treasure to your nation.

See your men as infant children and they will follow you into the deepest valley. See your men as beloved sons, and they will follow you to the death. But if a general is kind yet undisciplined, or loving but unclear with orders, unable to shake off his own confusion, then the knights will be as spoiled sons, impossible to employ.

If we know our soldiers' capabilities, but not the enemy's invulnerability, we will win only half the battles. If we know the enemy's vulnerability, but not our soldiers' weak spots, we will win only half the battles. If we know our soldiers' capabilities, and we also know the enemy's vulnerability, but do not realize the terrain does not favour battle, we will win only half the battles.

When the wise warrior moves, he is never at a loss. He strikes without doubts. And so it is said:

Know the enemy, and know yourself.

Win without danger.

Know Earth, and know Heaven.[3]

And you shall win every time.

---

3 'Know Heaven and Earth' if placed in the right position, suggests that 'Heaven and Earth' might be a better name for this chapter, in the sense that 'Earth' is the terrain, and 'Heaven' is the various other circumstances discussed.

CHAPTER ELEVEN

The Nine Situations[1]

---

1 This chapter is called *Jiu Di Bian*: the 'Nine Lands'. One might be forgiven for translating this, as in Chapter Ten, as 'Terrain', but while topography is certainly a feature, the meaning as discussed in the chapter is closer to what the modern military is more liable to term a 'situation'. My choice follows Giles (1910). Griffith (1963) favours 'varieties of ground', and notes that this chapter is more repetitive than most, and may have accidentally incorporated annotations into the main text. Perhaps in recognition of this, Sawyer (1993) uncompromisingly pushes for 'Terrain' in both chapter titles. Griffith amalgamates here two separate discussions on Situation that would otherwise seem repetitive, but I have left them as they are in Chinese, as I feel that the second set, later in the chapter, is intended to answer problems that Sun Tzu proposes after the first.

Master Sun says:

This is how war is waged.

Your situation may be:

- Compromised
- Liminal
- Contested
- Insecure
- Focal
- Committed
- Impeded
- Surrounded
- Mortal

When you do battle on the territory of a rival lord, your situation is Compromised.

When you enter his territory, but not too deeply, your situation is Liminal.

When both we and he might gain the upper hand, your situation is Contested.

Where we may occupy, but he may approach, your situation is Insecure.

When his lands are enclosed on three sides, and the first to arrive takes the multitude of All Under Heaven, then your situation is Focal.

When entering his territory so deeply that enemy forts and cities are at your rear, then your situation is Committed.

When mountains and forests, ridges and obstructions and boggy ground make it hard to march on the roads, your situation is Impeded.

When entry to territory is through narrow confines, and retreat is difficult, with our army vulnerable to attacks from his units, your situation is Surrounded.

Where only desperate battle keeps you from destruction, your situation is Mortal.

- When your situation is Compromised, do not fight.

- Where your situation is Liminal, do not halt.

- Where your situation is Contested, do not attack.

- Where your situation is Insecure, do not march onwards.

- Where your situation is Focal, make alliances.

- Where your situation is Committed, plunder.[2]

- Where your situation is Impeded, march on.

- Where your situation is Surrounded, make plans.

- Where your situation is Mortal, fight.

---

2 In other words, snatch supplies from close at hand instead of waiting for a relief force.

Since olden times it has been said that the skilled warrior made it impossible for the enemy's front and rear to communicate, impossible for his separate units to count on one another, impossible for his bold men to inspire his cowards, impossible for the officers and men to trust each other, impossible for his disrupted formations to re-form, impossible for his fighting soldiers to keep to their posts.

If your enemy needs to engage, make him redeploy. If he needs to move, make him stop.

If you ask me how you might prepare for the arrival of a well-organized enemy army, I would say: first seize that which he loves, then he will listen.

In war, speed is the key. Exploit your enemy if he is not ready. Take the road he does not watch. Attack the place he does not guard.

When occupying territory, this is the approach. To prevent the defending force from counterattacking, enter deeply. When food is in abundance, plunder, so that your army has sufficient provisions. Ration judiciously and do not overwork them. Build strength by uniting their spirits. Plan and implement your troop movements so that they are unpredictable.

Throw men into a place with no escape, with death more likely than retreat, and they will attack with all their might. Soldiers lose all fear when they lose all hope.

When there is no escape, they push back. When deep in enemy territory, they seize. When they have no choice left, they fight.

And so, without command, they will be vigilant. Without requests, they still do their best. Without promises, they are loyal. Without orders, they will be trusty.

Ban superstition and banish doubt, and they will go to death and beyond.

My soldiers are not rich, but they do not hate possessions. My soldiers are not immortal, but nor do they hate life. On the day the command comes to march out, they slump with tears on their collars. They lie on the ground with tears on their cheeks.

But throw them into a place with no escape, and they are as bold as Zhu and Gui.[3]

---

3 Here we have another reference specific to the state of Wu, but also another that is more likely to have been a popular story in Sun Tzu's supposed homeland. Zhuan Zhu was the name of the suicidal assassin commissioned by the future King Helü to kill his uncle. Cao Gui, also known as Cao Mo, was a seventh-century BC general from Lu who famously grabbed the Duke of Qi at a parley and threatened to slit his throat unless he withdrew his troops. The duke agreed, and was forced to keep his word by his fellow nobles. It is remarkably suspicious that Zhuan Zhu's name should have wormed its way into the 'thirteen chapters' that Helü claimed to have read only two years later.

The skilled warrior is like the *shuai-ran*, a snake found in the mountains of Heng. Strike at its head, and it lashes with its tail. Strike at its tail and it snaps with its head.[4]

---

4 The Hengshan (mountains of Heng) region had this name at the time of Sun Tzu. It was changed to Changshan around 179 BC, in order to avoid a taboo that prevented any proper nouns from aping the name of the incumbent emperor. Until the unearthing of the Yinqueshan manuscripts in 1972, all extant editions of the *Art of War* postdated 179 BC and hence used the new name. Some English translations made before the publication of the Yinqueshan manuscripts also restored the word *Heng*, on the understanding that the earliest manuscripts would probably have used it. The use of the word *Heng* in the Yinqueshan fragments was found to validate this theory.

If you ask me how you might steer an army into behaving like the *shuai-ran*, I say it is possible. The men of Wu and the men of Yue hate each other, but if they were in the same boat, cast adrift on the wind, they would help each other, as the left hand helps the right.[5]

---

5 The sudden decision to speak here of the 'men of Wu and the men of Yue' is interesting, as it implies that Sun Tzu is speaking now for an audience in Wu. As before, since the King of Wu welcomed Sun Tzu to his realm with the comment that he had read 'his thirteen chapters', this places the composition of the thirteen chapters in doubt, or at very least implies that Sun Tzu himself may have added material to the canonical thirteen before his death.

This might also explain the direct answers that Sun Tzu appears to be giving to offstage questions in this chapter. Perhaps this chapter summarizes an otherwise unidentified dialogue with the King of Wu. A Tang dynasty encyclopedia, compiled by the sometime *Art of War* critic Du You, included several passages purporting to come from just such a text. (See Ames 1993: pp. 199–223.)

And so, it has never been enough to trust in the securing of horses and the burying of chariot wheels. Make all courage as one in your management; that is the approach. Take hold of both the hard and soft; this is the principle in such situations.

And so the skilled warrior commands as if he is leading a single man by the hand. He leaves no choice.

The leader of an army should be calm and tranquil, straight and organized. He should keep his men unknowing, deceiving their eyes and ears. He should keep his men ignorant of changing plans and reverses in strategy. He should ensure that his men do not grasp changing positions and shifts in the odds.

When the time comes to lead, it is as if he climbs up high and kicks away the ladder. He plunges deep into enemy territory before going into action. He drives them on like a flock of sheep, driving them forward and back, though nobody knows where.

Assemble the military force, then throw them into jeopardy; such is the job of the general.

The Nine Situations vary; advantage changes with retreats and advances, and with principles of morale. This cannot be ignored.

When in enemy territory, this is the approach: go deeper for unity or risk desertions.

When leaving your kingdom and crossing the border, your forces come into a Compromised situation. When vulnerable from four sides, you are in an Insecure situation. When deep in enemy territory you are in a Committed situation. When you are only on the border, you are in a Liminal situation. When you have the enemy behind you and limited options, you are in a Surrounded situation. When you have no escape, your situation is Mortal.

- In a Compromised situation, we should make our will as one.

- In a Liminal situation, we should encourage fraternization.

- In a Contested situation, we should call in the reinforcements.

- In an Insecure situation, we should remain on the defensive.

- In a Focal situation, we should cultivate our allies.

- In a Committed situation, we should focus on our supply lines.

- In an Impeded situation, we should continue our advance.

- In a Surrounded situation, we should guard the choke-points.

- But in a Mortal situation, we should make it clear that there is no chance of survival. For it is in the nature of an army to push back when cornered. They obey when hemmed in.

He who does not know the strategies of a rival warlord cannot become his ally. He who does not know the dispositions of the mountains and forests, ridges and obstructions, or boggy ground, is unable to march his army.

He who does not use native guides is unable to use the terrain to his advantage.

He who forgets even one of these several points is unfit to command the army of a Hegemon.

When the army of a supreme monarch attacks a great kingdom, it is not possible to raise an army against him. For his reputation intimidates his foes, so that they do not unite against him.

Nor does he fight against fellow vassals of the Sovereign, nor does he scheme against them. His self-confidence and reputation intimidate his enemies. And so, their cities may be taken, and their kingdoms brought down.

Give out rewards unheeding of the rules. Give orders without rationale. Command your entire host as if managing a single individual. Give them their tasks, but do not give your reasons. Face them with the threat, but do not tell them of your advantages.

Thus they will survive a Compromised situation. Thus they will survive a Mortal situation. Confined and hard-pressed, they still snatch victory from defeat.

And so, in warfare, keep careful watch on what your foe is thinking. When the enemy is in your sights, you may kill a general from 1,000 *li*'s distance. We call this achievement through sheer cunning.

Thus, on the day that war is declared, shut down communications. Cancel passwords. Confine ambassadors. Be resolute in the council chamber, that you may achieve your goals. [6]

6 A 'password' in this case is actually *fu*, a tally. In ancient China, emissaries and commanders would each carry half of a charm or statuette, allowing for orders to be ratified by checking that the two halves matched.

When your enemy leaves an opening, be sure to go straight through it. First see what he loves, and conceal your timing. Bumble along as if blind, until the crucial moment of battle.

And so, at first, you should seem coy like a woman, so that the enemy opens the door. But then dart like a hare, and the enemy cannot hold you back.[7]

---

7 I have struggled with the expression 'coy like a woman'. Other translators have taken it even further, suggesting some sort of maidenly coquette, but the original text reads *ru chu nü* – 'like staying woman'. However, the word *nü* has the alternate meaning of 'weak and small' in Classical Chinese. So Sun Tzu either says 'be like a dithering woman', or 'be like a coy woman', or possibly simply 'appear indecisive, weak and small'. The question, then, is whether to translate the apparent sexism of Sun Tzu's phrasing, or to trust that it was the language itself that was sexist, not necessarily Sun Tzu's use of it – he did, after all, once legendarily command an all-girl platoon.

CHAPTER TWELVE

Incendiary Attacks[1]

---

1 The chapter on incendiary attacks is one of the shortest, and even in its current form appears to have been bulked out with material from elsewhere. Its latter phrases have nothing to do with incendiary attacks, and seem instead to wander off into a consideration of 'incendiary' in a more metaphorical sense. If we give Sun Tzu the benefit of the doubt, the later passages here extend the fire analogy, reminding the general of the irony in taking something he covets, only to destroy it in the process.

Master Sun says:

There are five forms of incendiary target.

- Humans
- Provisions
- Equipment
- Storehouses
- Military Units

Have good reason for setting a fire, and always have the tools to hand. There is a time for spreading fire. There is a day for starting it.

The time is when the weather is parched. The day is when the Moon is in the Winnowing Basket, the Wall, the Wings or the Axle. When the Moon is in these mansions, the wind rises during the day.[2]

---

2   For the Winnowing Basket, the Wall, the Wings or the Axle, the original has *ji bi yi zhen*, referring to ancient Chinese asterisms roughly equivalent to locations in Sagittarius, Pegasus, Crater/Hydra and Corvus. These are four of the twenty-eight Chinese lunar mansions: the parts of the sky traversed by the Moon during its monthly journey around the Earth. In other words, Sun Tzu advises that there are roughly four days in any given month ideal for setting fires. It is, however, unclear how the position of the Moon would influence this.

Generally, incendiary attacks can develop in five ways:

- When fire starts within his camp, quickly take action on his perimeter. But if fire spreads and his troops do not panic, wait and do not attack.

- When the fire is at its pinnacle, if you see an opportunity, take it. If you do not, then stay where you are.

- When fire starts on the perimeter, do not wait for it to spread within. Set fires at a good time.

- When fire starts upwind, do not attack downwind.

- Remember that wind endures by day, and ceases at night.

The soldier must be aware of these five incendiary variables, and bear them in mind.

And so, it is smart to use fire as an auxiliary attack. It is strong to use water. For water will cause him damage, but not destroy his *matériel*.

Sad is he who goes into battle, wins and conquers, yet does not reap the rewards of the victor. Fate calls this an opportunity wasted. And so it is said that the enlightened lord considers, but the good general manages.

Do not move without the advantage. Do not act without gain. Do not fight unless in peril.

The lord must not raise an army merely in anger. The general must not be provoked into battle.

Move if there is an advantage to engagement. If engagement brings no benefit, halt.

Rage may return to joy; anger may return to happiness. But a nation once destroyed may not be restored. The dead cannot be brought back to life.

And so the wise ruler is cautious, the good general is watchful, so to keep the kingdom safe and the army whole. Such is the way.

CHAPTER THIRTEEN

Espionage

Master Sun says:

When raising 100,000 men, and setting off on a march of 1,000 *li*, it is the common people who pay. The lord will need to find 1,000 pieces of gold per day. There will be unrest at home and abroad, beggars on the roads and lanes. Some 700,000 households will be unable to manage their affairs.[1]

---

1 Where I have 'common people' the original text has *bai xing*, the 'hundred surnames'. Where I have 'beggars', the original text has *dai*, 'neglected'.

A single day's battle might bring victory, but it could take years to bring that about. It is inhumane to undertake this, if you might know the enemy's state of mind for but a few hundred pieces of gold. Fail to do this, and you are no general, no aide to your ruler, no master of victory.

And so, the enlightened prince and the perceptive general use advance knowledge so that they move to bring victory, and their achievements surpass the multitude.

Advance knowledge cannot be found among ghosts and gods. It cannot be extrapolated from precedent. It cannot be calculated with experiments. Instead, it surely comes from men who know the enemy's state of mind.

And so, there are five types of spy to use:

- Native
- Embedded
- Double
- Dud
- Live

Use of these five tools leads to unknowable courses of action, and so it is called the Divine Thread. It is most precious to a prince.

A Native asset is a countryman of your enemy.

An Embedded asset is an officer in your enemy's administration.

A Double agent is an enemy spy that now works for you.

A Dud spy is one to whom we deliberately give false information, knowing he shall spread it to the enemy.

A Live spy returns with intelligence reports.

And so, in military affairs, your spies should be the ones you hold most dear, the ones most generously rewarded, and the ones whose tasks are most secret. You cannot use spies without great wisdom. You cannot use spies without great benevolence. You cannot obtain value from spies without accrued morsels of data.

Start small, in increments. There is no place where spies cannot be put to use.

If a spy's intelligence leaks before it is declassified, the spy and all he told must be put to death.

Where there is an army to strike, a city to attack, a person to kill, you must surely obtain advance knowledge of the defending general, his left- and right-hand men, his aides, his watchmen, and his bodyguards.

We must certainly send out our spies to discover these details. And certainly, we should expect that enemy agents will come to spy on us. By offering them bribes and asylum, we may turn them into spies that work instead for us.

Using their knowledge, we might recruit Native or Embedded agents to work for us.

Using their knowledge, we can put Dud spies to use with bad intelligence, and feed it to the enemy.[2]

Using this knowledge, Live spies can be sent into the field when the time is right.

---

2 Where I have 'Dud' and 'Live', the original text has *shi sheng*, 'dead and living'. Giles (1910) prefers 'Doomed' and 'Surviving', but at no point does Sun Tzu state outright that the former are sacrificial in nature, merely that they do not provide 'live' intelligence.

The ruler must be appraised of the roles of the five types of spy. This information must come from double agents, and hence the double agent can never be too greatly rewarded.

In ancient times, the Yin dynasty came to power because of Yi Zhi, of the Xia. The Zhou dynasty came to power because of Lu Ya, of the Yin.[3]

3 Both men were prominent ministers in their dynasties, who were instrumental in the foundation of the successor dynasties. Sun Tzu is suggesting that their power lay in their insider knowledge. Some critics have taken umbrage at the implication that they were 'spies' – Sun Tzu is probably more interested in their pivotal, embedded status.

And so the enlightened prince and the perceptive general should be ready to use the most wise of people as spies, so they can achieve great things. This is essential to the soldier. For when the military makes its move, it is where they have placed their trust.

The Life and Times of
The Art of War

In the centuries after the supposed composition date of *The Art of War*, the conflict between the various dukedoms escalated. Meanwhile, the Sovereign Son of Heaven's quasi-religious hold over his underlings continued to diminish. One by one, the dukes of the surviving states proclaimed themselves as kings in their own right, and whispers began to spread that their nominal overlord had lost the support of Heaven itself.

In an unexpected grand finale, a relatively young state rose to the top. The western land of Qin, a militaristic domain run on severe, autocratic lines, began a rapid expansion that soon gobbled up its neighbouring states. Although there were several attempts to curtail its power, the surviving rivals never quite managed to hold off its advance. The seven kingdoms dwindled, until soon they could be counted on the fingers of one hand. Another fell, and then another. And then there were none.

Qi, the Land of the Devout, alleged homeland of Sun Tzu, was the last rival to fall, in 221 BC. The victorious King of Qin proclaimed that he was now the true ruler of all under Heaven, and that consequently, he deserved a new title. He is remembered today as the First Emperor of China, and it was the discovery of his famous Terracotta Army in 1974 that has largely kept ancient Chinese military matters in the public eye for the last generation.

The First Emperor's role in the story of *The Art of War* is indirect. It comes in 213 BC, when he attempted to stifle debate, the citing of precedents and the dissemination of supposedly dangerous knowledge. In a nationwide mass burning of allegedly harmful manuscripts, the Qin authorities destroyed vast piles of classical Chinese books. Supposedly, the First Emperor kept single copies, even of forbidden works, in his own private library, but that, too, was burned when his dynasty fell only a few years later.

The action of the First Emperor was a watershed in the history of Chinese literature – a Year Zero that deprived posterity of countless ancient works. A handful of pre-imperial texts survived, and have been augmented in the centuries since by chance discoveries and archaeological findings. However, huge swathes of pre-imperial knowledge were irrevocably lost.

Recognizing the damage done to historical and scientific knowledge, scholars of the Han dynasty (206 BC–AD 220) attempted to reconstruct their knowledge of the past. It is from this period, for example, that we have *The Grand Scribe's Records* that give us the story of Sun Tzu's life, written centuries after the events they claim to describe.

Sun Tzu's supposed descendant Sun Bin was one of the victims of the tide of missing books. His *Military Methods* was lost in all but a few scattered fragments, until construction workers found a large portion of his text in an old grave at Yinqueshan (Silver Sparrow Mountain) in Shandong province in 1972.

The Yinqueshan Discovery

Archeologists at Yinqueshan unearthed a muddled stack of almost 5,000 bamboo strips, their bindings worn away, with some strips broken and others damaged by water. The strips contained a number of military manuals, and included pieces from the thirteen recognizable chapters of Sun Tzu's *The Art of War*, as well as works by Sun Bin and other military theorists. There was initial excitement at the belief that previously unknown fragments of both Sun Bin and Sun Tzu had been discovered in the tomb.

These are tantalizing new additions to a rich field of commentaries and anecdotes that have accreted around Sun Tzu. Interested readers are directed to Roger Ames' translation, *The Art of Warfare*, which includes both the original thirteen chapters of *The Art of War*, along with the ancillary material. It is undoubtedly of relevance to the broader world of Chinese military manuals, but may never have been intended as a true part of *The Art of War*, or possibly only formed that function among the officers of a particular clan, like a family bible with marginal notations, or a grandfather's forgotten memoirs, unearthed in an attic.

I have steered a middle ground with the new discoveries, omitting them from the main body of my translation, but instead summarizing them where relevant in the notes. This, I believe, accords them a reasonable degree of inclusion alongside the accepted Sun Tzu canon.

The archeologists who flocked to Yinqueshan also unearthed a relatively complete set of Sun Tzu's thirteen chapters, confirming for the first time that they already existed in this distinct form by the year 200 BC. Until

1972, this was a matter of some debate, as the oldest extant copy of Sun Tzu's *The Art of War* was only 1,000 years old, dating from the Song dynasty (AD 960–1279). Even then, the Song dynasty editor noted that he had some doubts about the integrity of the text.

One might say that the accretion of commentators over the centuries has helped obscure the fact that *The Art of War* is a flawed, fragmentary text. Where, one wonders, is Sun Tzu's promised chapter on 'Heaven' (Weather in my translation), alluded to in his introduction but never quite covered? Are we *sure* that certain passages, that seem to run off at a tangent, really ought to occupy the position that they do? When one strips away all the commentators and works through the *Art of War* as a single, unadorned text, one swiftly develops the impression that pieces of it are missing. Sun Tzu sets out his aims in an introduction, but then only elucidates *some* of his points. He spends some chapters talking in generalities, and others citing previous precedents and even previous authors.

It is, for example, strange that Sun Tzu should offer such insightful details on smoke trails from different troop movements, but make no mention at all of the effects of the seasons on military operations. In ancient, agrarian China, variations in the availability of men and vulnerability of a state were tied directly to

157

the time of year, and yet the extant text has not a word to say about it. It is equally odd that Sun Tzu should devote entire chapters to spies and incendiary warfare, but hardly ever mention archery, the use of crossbows or the requirements of charioteering.

Once a reader's nose is close to the text of *The Art of War*, its occasionally bitty, confused nature becomes apparent. Conjunctions like 'And so ...' appear in places as complete non sequiturs, implying that they are summarizing points now lost.[1] For much of the book that bears his name, Sun Tzu comes across as incisive, direct, blunt-spoken and experienced. But in several key passages, he suddenly wanders off the point, as if he has forgotten what he was talking about.

I do not believe this is Sun Tzu's fault. At some point in the life of his manuscript, the pieces have been mixed up. Maybe a crucial copy, source of many others, had a worn binding, causing at least one of its bundles to be restrung, possibly shoving certain pieces of text into the wrong place. Perhaps someone heard that the *The Art of War* had thirteen chapters and decided to fix it so that his personal copy matched the ancient tally.

---

1 See Mair, *The Art of War: Sun Zi's Military Methods*, pp. 32–3, and pp. 35–6 for statistical coverage of the manuscript's contradictions.

Or, someone with an incomplete set added a scroll or two to make their stack fit.

The temptation is immense to start cutting and pasting. In my earlier book on *Confucius* (Clements 2004), I deliberately rearranged my translations from *The Analects* into a chronological order, throwing the life of Confucius into sharp relief. But this is a translation of Sun Tzu *as we know it* and only obliquely relevant to his life story, not a redactive attempt to assemble where he might have been when he said it.

One previous translator did indeed succumb, shunting fragments of other texts into place in order to supply the passages that Sun Tzu *implies* should be there. Nor was his act necessarily a step too far – it is in the nature of classical authors to copy and quote each other at length, and the overzealous editor may indeed have accidentally *restored* passages, or approximations of them, to their rightful place. However, for it to be Sun Tzu's *The Art of War*, and not some other person's *The Art of War*, we have to work with what we have.

However, what we have is still fraught with problems.

Problems of Content

Doubts about the very existence of 'Sun Tzu' are nothing new. Since the eleventh century AD, Chinese scholars have disputed whether there could have ever been such a person.[2] In part, this is because there are valid doubts about his choice of subject matter, although it is still possible to steer a path through the arguments. It has been argued, for example, that Sun Tzu does not dwell on charioteering because his book is intended as an introduction to *infantry* warfare, then a relatively new development. At the time he wrote, the traditional chariot battles of China's central plain had become outmoded, particularly on the periphery, where jungles, forests and rocky ground made manoeuvre impossible. This, we might argue, is why Sun Tzu is so keen to specify the number of men who accompany a chariot, citing numbers of foot soldiers far in excess of the platoons that had accompanied vehicles in the preceding centuries.

Similarly, in largely ignoring divination and superstition, Sun Tzu would have been remarkably ahead of his time. But this is not necessarily impossible; his contemporary Confucius similarly occupied himself with the here and now, rather than thoughts of portents or prophecies.

Far more worrying to the scholar is the fact that Sun

---

2 Griffith, *Sun Tzu: The Art of War*, pp. 1–12, summarizes many of these issues.

Tzu should seemingly write, in the sixth century BC, about the duties of a 'general', when such a position was yet to be officially invented. At least as far as the annals of the Spring and Autumn Period describe wars and battles, the 'leader' of an army in the time of Sun Tzu would have been the duke himself. Such dukes might have advisers and consultants, but military operations were, at least officially, matters for the nobles. It was, in a sense, what nobles *did*, and the suggestion in *The Art of War* that a duke might sit at home in his palace while someone else marched off to battle does jar with the implications of the annals. It seems curiously pushy for Sun Tzu, a man of presumably low status, to start describing the duties of an appointed military leader, when his supposed era had no such thing. However, it is just as easy to argue that such military leaders were indeed commonplace, but merely forced to allow their superiors to take the credit. Do we not commit the same fallacies when discussing modern conflicts, by assigning a leader's personality to the troops he sends? Did George W. Bush, personally, *physically* invade Afghanistan? Or did he send someone else to do it? Similarly, when *The Grand Scribe's Records* says that 'Helü attacked Yue', surely there is some leeway in such a statement to assume that somewhere in his forces was an official who actually ran things?

There are other references in *The Art of War* that suggest it came from a later period. The use of the term Changshan, for a place that would have been called Hengshan in Sun Tzu's day, is attributable to later copyists desiring to avoid a taboo. But how many other references in the surviving texts are also the result of interfering scribes? When Sun Tzu refers to a cost of a 'thousand gold/metal' for running a military operation, is he referring specifically to metal coinage? Because if he is, he is being oddly anachronistic. But yet again, if a copyist is prepared to change the name of a mountain, perhaps someone was similarly willing to update the old book a little.

Even now, after the unearthing of the Yinqueshan document, our oldest edition of *The Art of War* is still a copy of a lost original. Even if the copy found in the Yinqueshan grave was already old when it was buried, it was still inscribed at least two centuries after the death of the man who supposedly wrote it. With such tenuous links to the past, it would only take a single busybody to 'help' readers understand his text by adding an anachronism. It is easy to make such mistakes; in fact, I have even left one deliberately in the final chapter of my translation ('Espionage') to demonstrate this.

'Dud' is given as my translation for *shi* ('dead') among Sun Tzu's list of the types of spy available. I chose the word for its punning closeness to 'dead', and for its original, early ninteenth-century meaning: 'one who is a failure, an incompetent, a weakling, a bore'.[3] But if archeologists dig up a fragment of this book in 2,000 years' time, and see the juxtaposition of 'dud' and 'live' on the same page, will some well-meaning critic misread it as a reference to ammunition, and hence unacceptably anachronistic? If English can change so much in a mere 100 years, that Lionel Giles's translation is practically unreadable, and my own 'dud' is vulnerable to misreadings, how much more might Chinese change in the intervening centuries?

Problems of Authorship

Let us imagine an old man in Shandong 2,000 years ago, sitting down and writing, for his own amusement, a work of fiction called *Sun Tzu's Secret Teachings*. Unearthed from his tomb long after his death, its cover missing and several of its slats broken or rotted, would this single scroll be heralded as a 'lost' Sun Tzu chapter? Probably. Would it be any less doubtful than some of the Sun Tzu material we already have? Possibly!

---

3   Green, *The Cassell Dictionary of Slang*, p. 377.

Perhaps the author of *The Art of War* was not the Sun Tzu who is name-checked a couple of times in the annals of Wu, and not mentioned at all in the annals of his home state of Qi. *The Art of War* still exists, whoever wrote it, just as arguments over Shakespeare cannot make *Hamlet* itself disappear.

Many of the problems of content mentioned above evaporate if the authorship of the text is dated just a century later, to a point where armies undoubtedly used the kind of technology that Sun Tzu describes, along with metal coinage. It cannot have been written too long after that, as *The Art of War* does not mention cavalry, which would have surely received a chapter to itself if the author were writing any later.

Which brings us to Sun Bin, the descendant, perhaps grandson of the legendary Sun Tzu, who also wrote a military manual. Perhaps Sun Bin was the author of *The Art of War* all along, and used his ancestor's name to impart a bit of traditional class to the manuscript. It certainly would not be the last time that a Chinese author had paid a predecessor the Confucian compliment of forging their work – in fact, many ancient Chinese texts may have gained implied weight by being attributed to an elder figure, more deserving of respect simply by seniority.

However, we do not know very much about Sun

Bin, either. He, too, warrants a mention in the *Grand Scribe's Records*, which describe him as a military man who was betrayed by a resentful colleague. As with Sun Tzu, his title is not his name: *bin* refers to a punitive mutilation from ancient China, in which the criminal was either deprived of his kneecaps, feet or toes. At some point in his career, Sun Bin was tattooed and maimed by the authorities, after being accused of some crime, real or imagined. Perhaps such an individual, fallen from favour, might well write up his ideas in an ancestor's name, hoping thereby to get around his own ostracism or shift the blame for unwelcome truths.

One of the few surviving stories of Sun Bin presents him at a horse race, guaranteeing his sponsor that he will win if he spreads his bets. Sun Bin ensures this by making sure that his worst horses compete against the rivals' best, but the best horses against the average, and the average against the worst. This ensures that his favoured horses win two-thirds of all their races, and while it is a nice story, it is hardly martial. However, Sun Bin is also named, explicitly, as being in the service of the King of Wei for over a decade, and being present at specific battles, so he has at least a marginally greater claim than his ancestor on truly existing. Most notably, although *The Grand Scribe's Records* begin by referring to him as Sun Bin, within a page it has renamed him

'Master Sun', and hence confused him irrevocably with his ancestor. Even in the book that established there was a Sun Wu and a Sun Bin in the first place, both are referred to as Sun Tzu![4]

Attempting to assign a strict, single identity to a Classical Chinese author can be a doomed venture. The groundbreaking scholars Bruce and Taeko Brooks, in an incisive analysis of the works of Confucius, raised so many questions about its authenticity that the text itself has lost almost all possible integrity. Their methods are all too readily applied to most other Classical Chinese works, to the extent that the authorship of *everything* is in doubt.

Brooks and Brooks are the fearless truth-speakers in the world of Classical Chinese studies, diligently breaking the original texts down until they reach a quantum level where nothing seems to fit. Their revolutionary deconstruction of *The Analects* of Confucius makes for a depressingly thorough read, relentlessly beating the romance out of the narrative of the philosopher's life,

---

4 Nienhauser et al., *The Grand Scribe's Records VII: The Memoirs of Pre-Han China*, pp. 39–40. Mair, *The Art of War: Sun Zi's Military Methods*, pp. 9–14 offers other suggestions as to the origins of Sun Tzu's name, and another fragment of supposed biography, although it was written 1,000 years after its subject's death.

and leaving the reliability of the surviving text in serious doubt. Confucius, we should now admit, did not 'write' *The Analects*; instead it was the result of many hands, writing long after the sage's death. Brooks and Brooks are similarly blunt and uncompromising in their assessment of Sun Wu, saying that he is 'wholly mythical' (Brooks and Brooks 2007). Instead, they suggest that the bulk of *The Art of War* is really the work of Sun Bin, amongst others, and that the use of the term *Sunzi* (Sun Tzu/Master Sun), a title rather than a given name, was deliberately intended to fudge the author's identity for ancient readerships. They even offer the suggestion that the thirteen chapters were actually composed between the years 345 BC and 272 BC, out of chronological order, beginning with chapter nine, and with the current 'first' chapter as the penultimate composition four decades later.[5]

One is left with an exasperating impasse, where Brooks and Brooks so successfully argue that nothing can be really believed, that the reader is ready to never open a book again – one hopes, one day, that a student of Brooks and Brooks will raise a hand in class and ask them to incontrovertibly prove they exist themselves,

---

5 See Mair, *The Art of War: Sun Zi's Military Methods*, p. 29.

and see how they like it! They are, however, power-ful, persuasive voices in modern Chinese studies that deserve to be considered.

Roger Ames, in his own translation of Sun Tzu, published even before the most stirring revelations of Brooks and Brooks, notes that a fixation on precisely *who* wrote an ancient book is an obsession of our own times. The *Art of War*, by 'Master Sun' has been quoted and consulted, contested and supported, for over 2,000 years. The influence and readership of the *Art of War* over the last 2,000 years does not evaporate simply because we are not sure who 'Master Sun' was.

The Yinqueshan discovery has confirmed that the thirteen chapters known to readers since medi-eval times were already extant in that form sometime around 200 BC. We might question who Sun Tzu really was, and indeed if he was a single person or a group of like-minded theorists. But Sun Tzu does not have to be the authority. The text itself is.

Much modern ink has become spilled over the rediscovery of the works of Sun Bin at Yinqueshan. But while it is indeed a groundbreaking addition to classical works, Sun Bin was not read for two millen-nia. His text disappeared centuries ago, and was not included in *The Seven Military Classics of Ancient China*, because nobody had a copy. Sun Bin might offer some interesting ideas or riffs on Sun Tzu, but we should really regard him as a 'new' author, with more of an influence today than at any time before 1972. Sun Bin had no influence on Khubilai Khan, or Chairman Mao, on Manchu invaders or samurai strategists, because nobody read Sun Bin for 2,000 years.

Similarly, while Yinqueshan offers us a tantalizing glimpse of some 'new' bits of Sun Tzu, it does not detract from the achievement of translations made before the Yinqueshan discovery. Samuel Griffith's 1963 version of the thirteen chapters is just as valid an account of the thirteen chapters as they were read in the Song dynasty, or Yuan dynasty, or Ming dynasty, as any other.

Perhaps tomorrow, archeologists somewhere in China will unearth a new stack of bamboo slats, offering us a more complete version of *The Art of War* than ever before. Perhaps it will even bear the telltale marks, in place-names and textual references, that mark it out as an older or more complete version. Should that day ever come, it might become easier for translators to raid Sun Bin's *Military Methods* for passages that could have been lifted from an earlier authority. Perhaps the documents found therein will offer more conclusive proof that Sun Bin was indeed the author of *The Art of War*, and that we should forget all about the legends of Sun Wu.

In a generation's time, perhaps Sun Bin's *Military Methods* will have become the default text for Chinese military thought, and 'Sun Tzu' a mere footnote. But legendary or not, Master Sun can endure a period away from the limelight. He has, after all, endured for more than two millennia already. Whoever he was, his book can still speak for itself.

Bibliography

Ames, Roger. *Sun-Tzu: The Art of Warfare – The First English Translation Incorporating the Recently Discovered Yin-Ch'üeh-shan Texts*. New York: Ballantine Books, 1993.

Balmforth, Edmund. 'A Chinese Military Strategist of the Warring States: Sun Bin', PhD thesis. New Brunswick, New Jersey: Rutgers, State University of New Jersey, 1979.

Brooks, E. Bruce. 'The Present State and Future Prospects of Pre-Han Text Studies' in *Sino-Platonic Papers* 46 (July): 1–74.

_____, and Taeko Brooks. *The Original Analects:*

Sayings of Confucius and his Successors. New York: Columbia University Press, 1997.

_____, 'An Overview of Classical Chinese Texts'. Amherst: University of Massachusetts, 2007. [Online: http://www.umass.edu/wsp/chronology/overview.html Accessed 16 September 2011]

_____, *The Emergence of China: From Confucius to the Empire*. Amherst: University of Massachusetts Press/Warring States Project, 2011.

Clements, Jonathan. *Confucius: A Biography*. Stroud: Sutton Publishing, 2004.

_____, *The First Emperor of China*. Stroud: Sutton Publishing, 2006.

_____, *Beijing: The Biography of a City*. Stroud: Sutton Publishing, 2008.

Dawson, Raymond. *A New Introduction to Classical Chinese*. Oxford: Clarendon Press, 1984.

Giles, Lionel. *Sun Tzu on the Art of War: The Oldest Military Treatise in the World*. London: Luzac and Co., 1910.

Graff, David. *Medieval Chinese Warfare 300–900*. London: Routledge, 2002.

Green, Jonathon. *The Cassell Dictionary of Slang*. London: Cassell, 1998.

Griffith, Samuel. *Sun Tzu: The Art of War*. New York: Oxford University Press, 1963.

Gu Di. *Sunzi Bingfa Da Cidian [Great Dictionary of Sun Tzu's Art of War]*. Shanghai: Shanghai Kexue Buji Chubanshe, 1994.

Kane, Thomas. *Ancient China on Postmodern War: Enduring ideas from the Chinese strategic tradition*. London: Routledge, 2007.

Knoblock, John and Jeffrey Riegel. *The Annals of Lü Buwei: A Complete Translation and Study*. Stanford: Stanford University Press, 2000.

Lorge, Peter (ed.). *Warfare in China to 1600*. Aldershot: Ashgate, 2005.

Mair, Victor. *The Art of War: Sun Zi's Military Methods*. New York: Columbia University Press, 2007.

Nienhauser, William, et al. *The Grand Scribe's Records: I: The Basic Annals of Pre-Han China by Ssu-ma*

Ch'ien. Bloomington: Indiana University Press, 1994.

_____, *The Grand Scribe's Records VI: The Hereditary Houses of Pre-Han China Part I by Ssu-ma Ch'ien*. Bloomington: Indiana University Press, 2006.

_____, *The Grand Scribe's Records VII: The Memoirs of Pre-Han China by Ssu-ma Ch'ien*. Bloomington: Indiana University Press, 1994.

Petersen, Jens Østergard. 'What's in a Name? On the Sources Concerning Sun Wu', in *Asia Major*, 3rd series (5.1), 1992. pp. 1–31.

Sawyer, Ralph, (with Mei-chün Sawyer). *The Seven Military Classics of Ancient China*. New York: Basic Books, 1993.

Tong Changlin. *Sun Wu Zi Moulue Leijie [Strategic Analysis of Sun Tzu]*. Beijing: Junshi Yiwen Chubanshe, 2007.

Zieger, Andrew. *Sun Tzu's Original Art of War: Sun Tzu Bing Fa Recovered From the Latest Archaeological Discoveries*. Vancouver: ColorsNetwork, 2010.

Chinese texts are readily available online for the main books cited.

For the *Art of War* itself:

http://ctext.org/art-of-war

For the biography of Sun Tzu from the *Shi Ji* (*Grand Scribe's Records*):

http://ctext.org/shiji/sun-zi-wu-qi-lie-zhuan

Acknowledgements

Leo Hollis at Constable & Robinson commissioned this book, and bravely fought for it on the frontlines of publishing. The library at London University's School of Oriental and African Studies provided the *matériel*. Seija Mäki-Kuutti, Raija Mäki-Kuutti and Ritva Parkkonen managed the home fires, in case of attacks by rival states. My wife, Kati Clements, was the support no general could do without. Andrew Deacon generously assessed my plans and debated my decisions, although any errors of deployment are my own.

THIS SCEPTRED ISLE
Christopher Lee

ISBN: 978-1-84529-994-1

What is Britishness? What allowed one small island group to rule a quarter of the world and, even today, to have the most spoken language after Chinese? What makes Americans admire the guts, traditions and loyalties of these island Anglo-Saxon and Celtic peoples? What is it that makes cynical Europeans and once-dominated Asians look to the British for opinion, literature, social norms and justice? The answers lie within the creation of British institutions, both commoner and aristocracy, during the past 2000 years.

Following the thought-provoking style of the original *This Sceptred Isle*, this new volume brings to life the character and frustrations so carefully studied by allies and enemies for twenty-one centuries – from Romans to al-Qaeda. Here Lee makes all the connections with institutions and changing industrial and social characteristics that even show us that Britishness is not exclusively British.

At a time when a major section of the British, the English, appear to be less and less sure who they are and who they are meant to be, *This Sceptred* Isle confirms who it is we really are.

WE SAW SPAIN DIE
Peter Preston

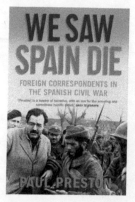

ISBN: 978-1-84529-946-0

From 1936 to 1939, the eyes of the world were fixed on the devastating Spanish conflict that drew both professional war correspondents and great writers. Ernest Hemingway, John Dos Passos, Josephine Herbst, Martha Gellhorn, W. H. Auden, Stephen Spender, Kim Philby, George Orwell, Arthur Koestler, Cyril Connolly, André Malraux, Antoine de Saint Exupéry and others wrote eloquently about the horrors they saw at first hand.

Together with many great and now largely forgotten journalists, they put their lives on the line, discarding a professionally dispassionate approach and keenly espousing the cause of the partisans. Facing censorship, they fought to expose the complacency with which the decision-makers of the West were appeasing Hitler and Mussolini. Many campaigned for the lifting of non-intervention, revealing the extent to which the Spanish Republic had been betrayed. Peter Preston's exhilarating account illuminates the moment when war correspondence came of age.

EMPIRE OF THE SUMMER MOON
S.C. Gwynne

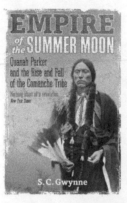

ISBN: 978-1-84901-703-9

Empire of the Summer Moon spans two astonishing stories. The first traces
the rise and fall of the Comanches, the most powerful Indian tribe in
American history. The second is the epic saga of the pioneer woman
Cynthia Ann Parker and her mixed-blood son Quanah, who became the
last and greatest chief of the Comanches.

Although readers may be more familiar with the tribal names Apache and Sioux, it was in fact
the legendary fighting ability of the Comanches that determined just how and when the
American West opened up. Comanche boys became adept bareback riders by age six; full
Comanche braves were considered the best horsemen who ever rode. They were so masterful
at war and so skillful with their arrows and lances that they stopped the northern drive of
colonial Spain from Mexico and halted the French expansion westward from Louisiana.
White settlers arriving in Texas from the eastern United States were surprised to find the
frontier being rolled backward by Comanches incensed by the invasion of their tribal lands.

Against this backdrop, Gwynne presents the compelling drama of Cynthia Ann Parker, a
nine-year-old girl who was kidnapped by Comanches in 1836. She grew to love her captors
and became infamous as the 'White Squaw' who refused to return, until her tragic capture by
Texas Rangers in 1860. More famous still was her son Quanah, a warrior who was never
defeated and whose guerrilla wars in the Texas Panhandle made him a legend.

S. C. Gwynne's account of these events is meticulously researched,
intellectually provocative, and, above all, thrillingly told.